First published in 2016 by:
Hasmita Shah

© Copyright 2016
Hasmita Shah

The right of Hasmita Shah to be identified as the author of this work has been asserted by her in accordance with the Copyright, Designs and Patents Act 1988.

All Rights Reserved
No reproduction, copy or transmission of this publication may be made without written permission. No paragraph of this publication may be reproduced, copied or transmitted save with the written permission or in accordance with the provisions of the Copyright Act 1956 (as amended).

ISBN: 978-1530253944

Dedication
This book is dedicated to my parents, Hansrajbhai and Gunvantiben, (Kaka and Ba) and also my uncle and aunt, Bapuji and Amritba whose courage, foresight and determination helped shape our destinies.

Acknowledgements
Thank you to Hitesh, my husband, for unfailingly supporting me in this endeavour and allowing me to pursue my own interests.

Thank you to my children, Nikhil and Arjun, as well as my nieces and nephews for inspiring me to write this book.

Thank you to my siblings and my cousins for encouraging me to finish this project.

Finally, thank you all for reading this, sharing it and helping to keep the memories alive.

Apologies
In undertaking this project, my intention was to document my parents' life history for future generations. I have completed this to the best of my ability and by consulting with family and friends after my parents' deaths but there may still be errors, inaccuracies, or omissions. Also I may have inadvertently offended someone in this book. For this, I apologise and humbly seek your forgiveness.
MICCHAMI DUKKADAM[1]

---

[1] If I have caused you offence in any way, knowingly or unknowingly, in thought, word or deed, then I seek your forgiveness

'Through the biography of her parents, Hasmita Shah gives us a moving but unsentimental account of the courage, sacrifices and spirit of a generation of Indians who remarkably crossed three continents remaking home. From the dusty bullock ploughed fields in the villages of Jamnagar District, Gujarat, to running a shop and dairy business in Fort Hall in the Kenyan highlands, to attempting to remake life back in India at the time of Kenyan independence, and finally working in a garment factory before setting up a corner shop in East London. This experience is shared by hundreds of thousands of people, not only from the same community, but – as the current panic over migration shows us - many more. We need many more books like this one.'

Alpa Shah, Associate Professor-Reader in Anthropology, London School of Economics. Author of *In the Shadows of the State: Indigenous Politics, Environmentalism and Insurgency in Jharkhand, India.*

CONTENTS

Foreword 2015	4
Family trees	8

Lest we forget

Preface 2007	11
India	16
Kenya	28
England	85
Kaka and Ba's legacy	161
Bapuji and Amritba's legacy	168
Tributes to Kaka and Ba	173
A short explanation of Jainism and a brief history of Oshwals	189
Glossary and sources	191

Foreword 2015

Growing up as a teenager in England, I am ashamed to admit that I didn't much care for my parents and was even embarrassed by them. I was the only Indian girl in my class (just one of 3 at Ilford County High for girls) and desperately wanted to be exactly like all the English girls so that I would be accepted as one of them. My older sisters took on the guardian role and represented my parents at any parents evening or at other school functions. I was jealous of my friends who would go shopping with their mums and talk to them as their best friend. I barely spoke to my mum and was rarely seen out in public with her, not that difficult as she rarely went out; my dad did all the shopping so there was no need for her to step out of the house. I was embarrassed that my parents spoke so little English and that created a language as well as a social barrier. Although I spoke Gujarati, it was kitchen Gujarati, the kind of language for everyday use, not for having esoteric debates and long philosophical discussions. I considered English to be my first language, and I wanted to adopt all things English.

Even at Reading where I went to university, I never invited my parents to come and visit me, nor when I was in Montpellier, France for my year abroad. When I graduated, I invited Hitesh and my sister Bena and her husband for the graduation ceremony. Why didn't I invite my parents? I never even considered it! And they never asked or questioned these things but tacitly accepted my decisions. Did they mind? I really don't know. We both accepted that I was educated, they were not. They just didn't expect to interfere with my studies and left me to get on with my life.

Yet they wanted us to get the best education possible. They who had had so little education, wanted all of us including the 4 girls to finish our studies, go to college, maybe even university. Education, they believed was the panacea, the escape from the drudgery and toil that they had had to suffer to make ends meet. If we were educated, we would get good jobs and a stable income.

So they toiled even harder in order to send my elder sisters (Niru, and later Manjula and Bena) to England at a tender age to study. In the end we all moved to England so that my brother Shailesh and I could also get a decent education. Ironically, in educating ourselves, we drifted further away from our parents, at least I did. I barely spoke to them, yet they continued to do everything for me. I just selfishly took and they kept giving with a smile.

It is only after I had children of my own, that I came to appreciate the true worth of my parents. Suddenly I realised that I may not have much more time with them and I was not ready to let them go. As they became more independent, I started to desperately cling on to them as if my existence depended on them. I wanted to make up for lost time.

So I decided to take some time off from work in 2007 and embark on a journey to find out about their lives, to find out what trials and tribulations they faced. Whilst not a unique story, I wanted to record their unique lives as a permanent record of our family's history for my children. Maybe I was hoping that the process of writing would have a cathartic effect upon me and I would be freed from the burden of guilt for my selfish and inconsiderate youth.

I spent a number of hours with Kaka and Ba, especially Kaka to learn about their early lives. Unfortunately I did not finish writing this at the time and after I went back to work, had 2 cataract operations, somehow the project kept being put off. In early 2009, I started to try and finish this with an urgency as Kaka was diagnosed with cancer in late 2008. However alas, work and other things took over and I barely wrote one chapter. After April, Kaka's health deteriorated rapidly and the once strong man who had brought me 2 heavy bags of fruit and vegetables to take home, could barely walk. I could not believe that Kaka who had never really smoked, who had never drunk any alcohol, who had been a vegetarian all his life and had eaten only freshly cooked home foods, could be diagnosed with cancer. And that too, aggressive stomach cancer.

Kaka who had never been ill his whole life was now reduced to a state of complete helplessness, reliant on others to move him from bed to wheelchair, to dress him and wash him. By mid-May we had all accepted the inevitable as to watch him deteriorate so rapidly was traumatic on all of us. And yet throughout all of this he remained mentally alert and accepted his fate with equanimity. Not once did he complain or shout at us or otherwise show his frustration or anger.

He eventually died peacefully on 5th June 2009 at home, having been visited by hundreds of relatives, friends and well-wishers over the last few months and having met his great grandson for the first time.
And so I was left to complete this book without Kaka's additional input, without him witnessing what I'd written so far. It was going to be a difficult task not just emotionally but also because Kaka had such a fantastic memory about his past.

And yet even after his death, he kept encouraging me. The day of his death, I was trying to write something for the *sadadi*[2] and picked up an old A4 diary that he had. He had lots of these old diaries at home as they had previously owned a stationery shop in Upton Park and any unsold previous year diaries would be brought home to use for writing or as address books. I was trying to draw up a timeline of events and ascertain the year that my *Motiba*[3] had passed away. Imagine my surprise when I flicked through this diary and found all of our birthdates, our cousins' birthdates and my aunt, uncle and *Motiba's* birth and death dates all in Kaka's wonderfully illegible writing. Incredible! I could have picked up any one of a dozen diaries and somehow I picked this particular one. Was it a sign? I certainly thought so and I hoped that Kaka wherever he was, would keep encouraging me and pushing me to finish this book. I owed it to him. I wanted his memory to be forever etched in our minds. I had chosen the title of this book 'Lest we forget' when I first started writing this book. It could not have been a more appropriate title and I wanted to make sure that I finished this quickly lest I forgot.

Unfortunately the years passed and still this book was incomplete. Almost 3 years later Ba passed away and again I resolved to finish this project. It is now over 3 years since Ba passed away and I'm finally seeing the light at the end of the tunnel. It has been a long labour of love. Not because it was difficult to write but simply because I kept putting it off; other tasks appeared more pressing. I hope that this book will serve to educate all of Ba and Kaka's grandchildren and their children as to their roots, their rich heritage and culture and as to their principles, their values and the sacrifices they made so that we, their children and our children, are all able to enjoy a better life. I hope that in years to come these children will appreciate this effort and it will provide them with an insight of how far we have come within a generation in terms of wealth and education but also I hope that it will serve to remind everyone of the core values and principles that were so ingrained in Kaka and Ba. I hope these are never lost and that their legacy continues into the future generations. Kaka and Ba used to remind us about not forgetting our parents. They frequently used to sing that *bhajan*[4] to us. I tried to find an English translation of the *bhajan* but to no avail and so I have translated it myself trying to remain faithful to the poetic lyrics of the original. The words are extremely poignant and it is one of my favourites as I feel this was written specially for my parents.

---

[2] Prayer meeting (following a death)
[3] Paternal grandmother

[4] Religious song

Forget All Else But Never Forget Your Parents

You can forget everything else but don't forget your parents
Don't ignore their countless virtues, they are your very essence
They worshipped stones to the ends of the earth to see your face
Don't turn your heart into stone and crush these souls' spirit and grace
Feeding tiny morsels, they've lovingly raised you, remember
Never spit poison at those that nourished you with nectar
Cuddling you a million times they've fulfilled your every desire
To those that quenched your thirst, don't ever extinguish their fire
You may be earning millions but what use is all that cash
If you can't make them happy, this is not wealth but simply ash

If you want to protect your lineage, look after your parentage
What you sow is what you reap, heed this old adage
Sleeping on the wet patch they would lay you where it was dry
Don't forget all this and never make those beloved eyes cry
They lovingly paved your path with flowers so fragrant
Don't stab that precious love with thorns by being arrogant
Wealth will buy you everything except your mother and father
So worship their holy feet and respect them like no other

Ba and Kaka at a Swaminarayan temple in Tithal, Gujarat

Raishibhai and Hiraben's (Ba and Amritba's parents) family

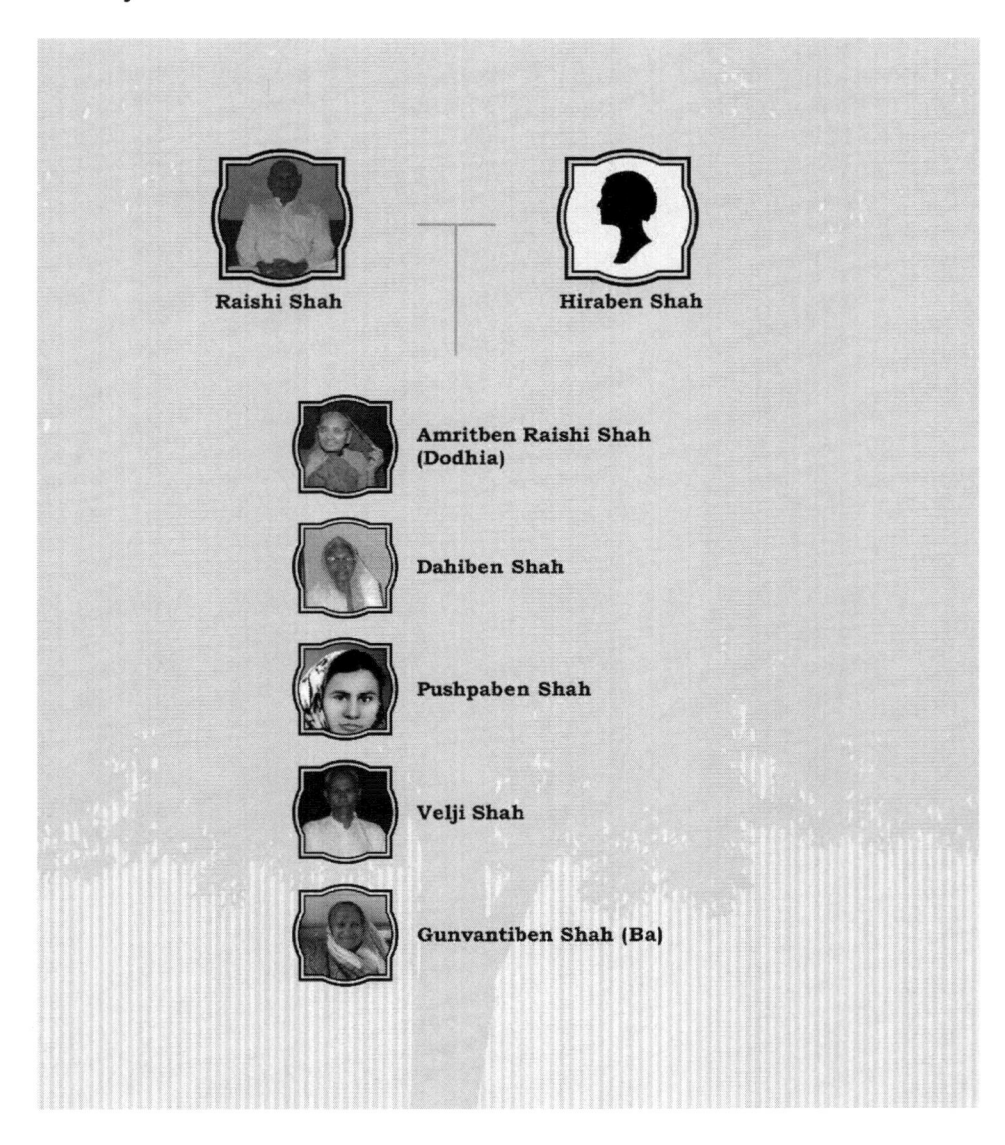

Raishi Shah — **Hiraben Shah**

- Amritben Raishi Shah (Dodhia)
- Dahiben Shah
- Pushpaben Shah
- Velji Shah
- Gunvantiben Shah (Ba)

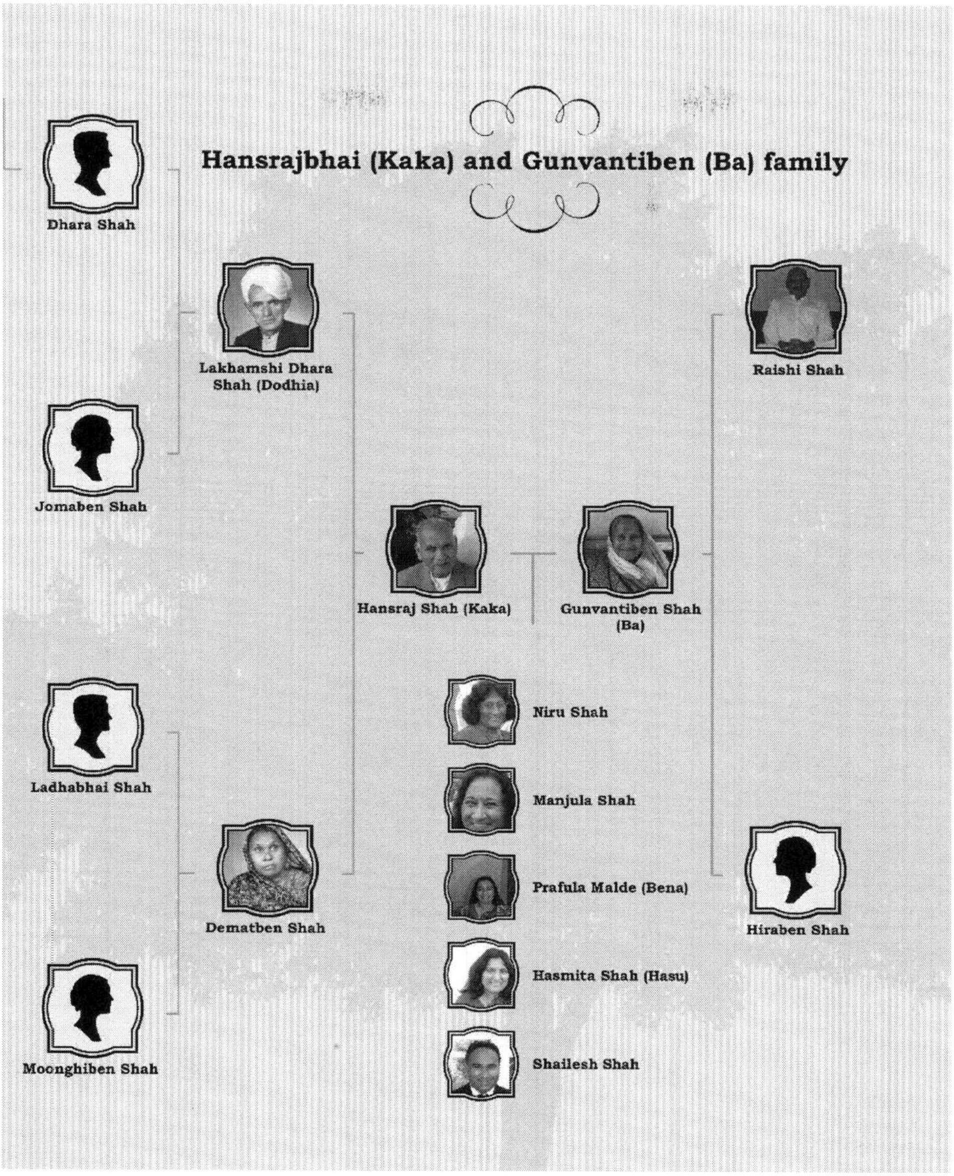

Hansrajbhai (Kaka) and Gunvantiben (Ba) family

- Dhara Shah
  - Lakhamshi Dhara Shah (Dodhia)
- Jomaben Shah
- Ladhabhai Shah
  - Dematben Shah
- Moonghiben Shah

Hansraj Shah (Kaka) & Gunvantiben Shah (Ba)

Children:
- Niru Shah
- Manjula Shah
- Prafula Malde (Bena)
- Hasmita Shah (Hasu)
- Shailesh Shah

- Raishi Shah
- Hiraben Shah

Raishibhai (Bapuji) and Amritben (Amritba) family

Lakhamshi Dhara Shah (Dodhia)

Raishi Lakhamshi Shah (Bapuji)

Amritben Raishi Shah (Amritba)

Raishi Shah

Dematben Shah

- Zaverchand R Shah (Zavbhai)
- Dinuben Shah 
- Shantaben Shah (Shantu) 
- Gulab Shah 
- Ansuya Shah
- Sunita Shah 
- Dilip Raishi Shah (Dodhia) 

Hiraben Shah

Lest We Forget

Preface 2007

Who are my parents?

Half past seven in the morning and the shrill ring of the telephone wakes me up suddenly. I've overslept again and now I have to spend a few precious minutes talking to Kaka who's asking what I want today from the market. 'Some apples perhaps'- I still haven't used up the last ones. 'OK then maybe some clementines'. 'What about mangoes? The last ones were really sweet'. I haven't the heart or time to tell him that we still haven't finished the last lot. 'Ok good and I'll bring some peppers and lemons as well. What time are you free? Ok I'll bring it to work at around 3pm.'

He would not have understood why we hadn't eaten the last lot of mangoes. What are you eating, he would ask. The fact that he'd brought those only 3 days ago and you can hardly eat six mangoes in 3 days is beyond his comprehension. There's 4 of us. I could always make mango juice. Mango is the king of fruits. I hope he's not bringing more fruit,' says Hitesh. 'Yes he is. It's Ok. He'll bring it to work and I'll pass it to Bena'

The receptionist rings up in the afternoon to let me know my dad is here to see me. He's now a well-known face downstairs. I walk downstairs. He's sitting on the sofa with 2 carrier bags on the table. 'Hello, how are you? ' 'Fine'. There's 2 bags - some apples, pears, cucumber, lemons, peppers and mangoes. Oh and your mum sent some fresh orange juice and some *rotlo*[5]. Bena wanted the apples and pears and share the rest with her'

'Ok I'm off then. I'll try and go to the market again and see whether they have any more mangoes.'

I can't understand why he has to make so many trips to the market and get so much fruit most of which is given away. But mine is not to reason why. Mine is to accept the fruit that my father gets so much pleasure out of giving. A minute later, he says thank you to the security at reception and trundles off. I take the lift up carrying 2 heavy double wrapped Sainsbury's bags full of fruit.

---

[5] Millet chapatti

'I see the Red Cross has arrived' says Tony as I stagger back to my desk again with the shopping. It is a standing joke at work that my dad does all my shopping. I have to confess that I've probably bought lemons only a couple of times in the last ten years. Otherwise Kaka brings them. And we go through a lot of lemons. I drink the fresh orange juice that my mum has sent me; it tastes really delicious and I take a moment to reflect on Kaka and Ba.

Kaka and Ba, my parents who are now nearing the end of their seventies. Ba is 77 and Kaka is 79; both are more energetic than me. Kaka will bring in 2 heavy bags of shopping for me at work and I will complain to him afterwards that it was too heavy for me to carry on the tube. Ba only eats one meal a day but if we say we're coming to Ilford where they live, she'll make so much food, that we have to take most of it home and eat it the following day.

They get so excited if I tell them we're coming to Ilford. They'll start planning what food to make and Kaka will plan all the shopping that he can get, because we'll have the car and so no need to restrict to 2 bags! And he thinks about all the other relations and friends living nearby who he can give a few mangoes or other fruits to. So that week he'll make several trips to different markets, 2 or 3 in the same day to bring the maximum quantity of fruits that we can take and distribute in Harrow, where Bena and I live.

We hardly ever get to Ilford. Work and life gets in the way. Weekends are usually spent taking the boys to their various sporting commitments and weekdays are just too tiring to go all the way to Ilford to visit.
So they come over, they understand. Never mind that they have to change trains a couple of times and take a bus as well from their house to the station. And of course they never come empty handed. Kaka will bring at least 2 bags of shopping when he comes.

They'll usually come to visit other people and use my house, so conveniently located by the station, as a first stop. They'll drop the shopping and a minute or so later, be on their way. Usually I'm not even home, I'm at work but he has a key. They tend to come after lunch and then after they've done their rounds, will try and wait for me to come back from work and see me for a few minutes before they make their long journey back home.

One of many *bhajan* sessions

They will try and get to all their social commitments and have a more hectic social life than we do. Most of it is spent going to everyone's *sadadis* to pay their respects and funerals. I used to think that all their peers and friends dying would make them sad but they're very philosophical about these things and tend to accept death as an old familiar friend. In Jain philosophy death is a comma, a transition to the next stage and not a full stop.

In their twilight years, they have been doing so much for everyone. Not just me or their other children, but everyone they meet, they are touching them in a special way and I feel so privileged to call them my parents. They make a funny couple, my dad almost 6 ft. and walking briskly and my mum under 4'11 trailing well behind. 'Who arranged this match? ' ask my children. I shrug my shoulders and respond I don't know.

I don't know who they are and where they've come from. They are my parents but I know so little about them. I feel ashamed. So wrapped up in my own life and selfishly taking everything that is given, I really have not bothered to find out about them. I do not want to wake up one day and regret that I never asked them about their childhood, their youth.

I want to find out more about Kaka, Hansraj, the king of swans, translated literally. He is very elegant and regal, always taking care with his appearance. His favourite pastime is shopping, but shopping for fruit and vegetables most of which is given away; he also loves travelling and meeting new people and loves singing *bhajan*s so we have to cajole the grandchildren into having a *bhajan* session every so often as it gives him so much pleasure. And of course I have to mention his passion for *bhukhar*[6]. He looks forward to all the bank holidays when he can invite us all round for dinner and then hopefully we'll stay till late and play *bhukhar*. If he's visiting someone or if they come round, he'll usually be nodding off whilst they're still talking, but get him involved in a game of *bhukhar* and he'll be happily playing till 2 or 3 in the morning.

One of our many late night *bhukhar* sessions

And why is it that I call my father *kaka*[7] and my uncle *bapuji*[8]? The reason given to me was that we copied our elder cousins to whom, Kaka was *kaka*. But they call my mum *masi*[9], yet I call her *ba*[10]. Well Ba would not accept us calling her *masi* and made us call her Ba. So I had 2 women I call Ba – My mum and my Bapuji's wife (who I will call Amritba) who also happened to be my mother's sister as 2 brothers married 2 sisters.

---

[6] Indian card game

[7] Uncle(father's brother)
[8] Father
[9] Aunt (mother's sister)
[10] Mother

I want to find out more about Ba, Gunvanti, full of virtues, translated literally, which she truly is. But she is also the stubborn, and obstinate lady who drives us all crazy with her steadfast resolves.

Over the last decade, she has been prescribed tablets for high blood pressure, cholesterol, her heart, and thyroid. Some tablets had to be taken in the evening, but she would not let even a glass of water pass her lips, after her meal. All food and drink are only taken at the time of her meal, so she would have all the tablets together. Of course having the tablets themselves was the subject of various debates. For someone who'd never taken a tablet for a headache, the thought of taking so many was anathema to her and she had frequently talked about not taking any tablets. Emboldened by the support of her brother (equally stubborn and obstinate) following her recent trip to India, she has now stopped taking all tablets, despite our numerous protests. Following a heated debate about her intake of salt, she has now given up salt. Despite living in England for the last 36 years, she can barely string a sentence together in English. I, who love languages certainly did not inherit any of my linguistic abilities from her. But if I had half her resolve! I want to find out more about this fascinating lady, who challenges us every day, that I call Ba.

My parents' story is not unique. It is virtually the same story for all the Indians who migrated from India to Kenya and then the UK in search of better opportunities. Nonetheless, the story is a remarkable story. A story of how lives have been transformed completely within a generation or two; a rags to riches story, from having nothing to having it all, a story of the uneducated and illiterate parents producing some of the most highly educated offspring; but together with this, a story of displacement, of not belonging, of losing one's identity with nowhere to really call home.

India

Navagam (our house was at the end); *derasar*[11] at the back

Kaka's childhood

Kaka, Hansraj, was born in 1927 in Navagam, a small village about 15 miles south west of Jamnagar, in Gujarat. According to the passport, he was born on 25 August, but that could be incorrect as they didn't have registrations of births in those days. By remembering the season he was born and how old others were at the time of his birth, the passport date has been estimated. Some people's passports were deliberately doctored to show they were older or younger for certain reasons, however Kaka reckoned his passport age was fairly accurate

A history of Navagam has been written by the late Somchand Ladhabhai Gudka who was also born in Navagam in 1913. According to his article, Navagam, literally meaning new village, was founded around 1850 when 3 families, one of whom was my great great grandfather Nongha Dedhar Dodhia, decided to settle there and form a new village.
A formal opening ceremony was performed in 1852. Soon other *Oshwals*[12] settled in Navagam from neighbouring villages as well as Jamnagar and the village also attracted skilled labour from other communities, such that the village boasted a carpenter, a potter, a blacksmith, a goldsmith, a cobbler, a tailor and even a shepherd. The main activity and mode of living was farming. In those days, farming

---

[11] Jain temple

[12] Jain community originating from Halar in India

was done manually and by using bullocks for pulling the ploughs. Heavy physical work meant there was little time for other activities. In any case the absence of organised forms of entertainment such as cinema or television meant people would usually sit and socialise if there was free time in the evenings. From other accounts of life in the villages, it appears that from time to time visiting troupes of entertainers came to the villages to perform shows, circus type acts and recite folk lore. This was a rare treat and Kaka did not recollect any such entertainment.

The family were reasonably well off when Kaka was born. His grandmother had already passed away prior to his birth and his grandfather died just a few days after Kaka's birth. His grandfather had been a headman of the village and was well respected in the village.According to the articles on Navagam, Kaka's grandfather and his grandfather's brother, as heads of the village, were instrumental in defending the village from 2 notorious bandits and their gang that used to loot and plunder neighbouring villages. These bandits would come in the evenings when the cows were being herded home, hiding behind these sacred animals.When they came to Navagam, Dharabhai (Kaka's grandfather) and Deparbhai (Kaka's grandfather's brother) got the villagers organised by getting everyone on the rooftops; from there they hit the bandits with tiles.

During this fight, one of the bandits was killed and the others fled leaving their gun and sword behind. The gun was handed over to the Government but the sword was kept for some time by one of the *Oshwal* community and Kaka said he had seen this sword.

My great grandfather and his brother were congratulated personally by the ruler of Jamnagar and as a mark of respect they were garlanded with turbans. The rulers of Jamnagar had been unable to catch these bandits until the Dodhia brothers defeated them. As a result of this when he was a small boy, Kaka's father had to lie about which village he came from. Since other bandits were seeking revenge for this defeat by Navagam, to say you were from Navagam would be risking your life. But even these bandits had some scruples. They never harassed any women and some of them even regarded some ladies as sisters who they would protect from anyone and everyone.

Kaka only had one brother, Raishi (I've always called him Bapuji) who was about 8 years older than Kaka. There had been another 5 siblings (4 sisters and one brother) who unfortunately had passed away as babies or toddlers. Medical care and sanitation was always a problem such that it was accepted that more than half the children born would not make it beyond the first few years. Kaka's father, however had 10 siblings, (7 brothers and 3 sisters) of whom at least 7 survived and had children themselves. His mother also came from a large family of seven brothers and 3 sisters including herself. In turn these aunts and uncles had a few children each, so Kaka had numerous cousins, many of whom were his age or older and a lot of them lived in Fort Hall.

Both parents would be busy working – either in the fields or in the kitchen and so it was left for the children to look after their siblings and themselves from a very young age and also provide their own pastimes. No Nintendo's or PS2 during those days!

The children would invent their own games, usually only the boys as the girls would be required to help in the kitchens from a much earlier age. Mostly they would play some form of hide and seek or catch. With no adult supervision, these activities were not without their hazards. Kaka recounted an incident when they were all playing a game with a stick around a peepul tree. Whoever had the stick had to avoid getting caught and so the boy with the stick climbed up this tree. Unfortunately he missed his footing and fell. With no medical care available in the village, and not realising the state of his injuries, his parents gave him some milk which aggravated his internal injuries and by the next morning he had died.

In another incident that Kaka recounted to me, one of his cousins and a friend fell down the village well. They were looking down the well, which some workers were making deeper and they must have leant so far forward that they fell in. Lucky for them that these workers were there to rescue them. These incidents show that even in these times, life was full of hazards. However, if incidents happened, they were accepted as part of one's destiny, one's fate and so there was never a question of attributing blame.

Village life revolved around the *otlo*[13] usually situated in the middle of the village. This is where the elders, usually men, would gather for a chat, discuss matters and relax after the day's work.

When Kaka was around 4 years old the family went to Mumbai and here they had 3 grain shops. Bapuji who was 12 years old used to manage one of the shops, Kaka's father managed the second, whilst the third was

---

[13] A seating area in the centre of the village, usually with a tree in the middle. This would be the centre point where people would congregate for a chat.

managed by an employee. They were reasonably affluent, however their living conditions were fairly basic. They lived near Parel, the whole family sleeping and cooking in the one room, with a block for toilets and a bathroom to be shared by all the other 40 lodgers. The family used to go to the beach near Prabhadevi quite often.

Kaka went to a school called Chich Pokly School - on our trip to India in 2006/2007, he pointed out the area and he mentioned to the driver the name of the school but alas the school is no more!

Once when he was a few years old, Kaka became severely ill and could not eat anything for over 2 weeks, but slowly recovered. When Kaka was around 5, he got bitten on the lips by a big rat whilst sleeping. Rats were quite prominent in India.

Ba always burst out laughing when she heard this story. I couldn't understand how she could be so amused. She couldn't understand how his lip could have got bitten – a leg perhaps but the lip? No, she was reduced to hysterics.

Unfortunately the shops were not doing well. On the advice of a well-meaning relative, they had decided to purchase a lorry to transport grains from the market. The relative had driven in Kenya and said he would drive the lorry but on the first day he decided he couldn't cope with the Mumbai traffic! So they had to employ someone else. Their expenses were high and the accounts were not kept in good order, so sadly in a short time they became bankrupt. At 7, Kaka and the family came back to Navagam, having got heavily into debt. 5 years before Kaka's birth, in 1922, his father had also gone to Kenya to try and make it there, with the intention to settle there and call his family members later on. However, he found it difficult to settle there and returned back to Navagam.

In Navagam, Kaka continued to go to school but also worked in the fields. The school was a government school and free, so he would go regularly unless he was required in the fields during the day, in which case there was no problem about bunking off. In any case the schooling was rudimentary and only for a few hours so he would still be required to do his chores in the early morning or in the evenings. The family used to grow radishes, garlic, peanuts, millet and other vegetables. Kaka would have to walk miles to go and sell these to other villages, or to traders in Jamnagar, particularly the peanuts.

The problem with farming was that there was no irrigation system and you had to rely on rainfall. Navagam being on the periphery of the monsoon belt received an irregular rainfall which was often below normal. In addition to famine which lasted more than 1/3 of the year, a number of major epidemics and natural disasters such as cyclones, locusts and flood caused considerable hardship.

The family had a few plots of land but they were scattered far and wide so to tend to all of them carefully was also difficult. Sometimes my grandfather would have to stay overnight to tend to the crops and Kaka would go there after school to take him food and maybe spend the night there if required. The family also had a *wadi*[14]- here there would be a well but this was to be shared by all the villagers so there was a rota for taking water, usually you could water your *wadi* a couple of times a week.

My grandfather although hard working, was not very organised and efficient. So anyone he employed would take advantage of him and with the plots of land being quite far away from each other, it was difficult to keep a careful eye on all the crops. My grandfather also had 2 addictions, tobacco and tea. He would often procure these items on credit so any harvest would have to wipe off these debts first. In particularly hard times if there was a shortage of rains and poor harvest, they would have to drink tea without milk and sugar. Kaka recounted in his journal how they would go begging for yogurt or *chaas* and if lucky would get a little from a few houses, otherwise they were reduced to eating dry *rotlo* without the luxury of *chaas*; he often went to bed hungry.

Times were really really hard. Any harvest would be taken by the creditors (mostly shop owners who had let them buy goods on credit) so that eventually there would be nothing left and they would yet again have to buy food, even grains on credit at a higher price. So they were caught in this vicious spiral of debt. They owed 600 rupees (about £8) to a fellow *Oshwal* who took them to court as they had not repaid the money on time. The court case was in a different village and therefore more precious time was taken to attend at the trial. The court ruled in favour of the plaintiff, but they did not have the means to repay the debt.

I asked Kaka whether the other party had all the paperwork to prove that this money was owed to him. No, but there was no denying the fact that he was owed this money. In those days your word was as good as your bond. So to lie and deny the money was owed would have been unthinkable. Debts were always acknowledged and repaid and even this debt was eventually repaid when Bapuji used to send money from

---

[14] Field for growing vegetables

Kenya. Bapuji already married in 1932, at the age of 12, was taken to Kenya around 1936 by one of his uncles.

Farming was a precarious business. Every few years, the rains would fail to come and there would be no harvest. The family already poor and heavily in debt would again have to borrow money or rely on the charity of others to survive. It was the same for most of the community and so at the beginning of the century some people had begun venturing to Africa – 'the Dark Continent.' Most had endured extreme hardships and risked their lives in getting there in the early days by dhows. Once there they had to deal with a foreign place, a new language, extreme loneliness. But it was a fertile land and there was money to be made if you worked hard. So it was that Bapuji, a young teenager, left his parents, his only brother, his young wife (Amritba) and baby (Zavbhai) in 1936 to come to Kenya, to make something of himself and to support his family.

Those who remained behind in India, including Kaka carried on for a few more years, living on the edge, not knowing where their next meal was coming from but surviving from one day to another. For Amritba and Bapuji, their first born child Ratilalbhai had already passed away at around a year old, probably due to pneumonia.

Even Zavbhai, aged 2 fell severely ill with pneumonia to the point where there was no hope left. Bapuji was in Kenya, but Amritba was not about to let her second child die. She nursed him back to health keeping his chest warm and miraculously he survived. Zavbhai must have been in the throes of death, as Kaka wrote in his journal that Zavbhai had received a new *avatar*[15], he had been born again.

And then again disaster struck! In 1939/40 there was a severe drought in Navagam and therefore no harvest. They literally had no food and no money. All the cattle in the village were dying as there was no water or grass to feed upon. One of Kaka's maternal uncle took pity upon them and invited the family over to his village, Khara Beraja. Here, his uncle said they had enough water and they would be able to eke out a living. They, (Kaka, his parents, Amritba and Zavbhai) stayed here for one and half years with his uncle's family in a 2 room house. Khara Beraja is near the sea and the ladies used to go and collect something called *cher*[16]. They would feed this to the cattle as they did not have the luxury of grass. They also used to grow and sell chillies and Kaka used to go to

---

[15] Life form

[16] Leaves of trees that used to grow by the sea

Bunghe, a village 3-4 miles away to sell milk. He would wake up early around 5am and then go and sell milk. The milk would be carried on a *kavad*[17]. Kaka said he got paid weekly for this. After this he would come back and go to school for a full day from 9am till 5pm.

Khara Beraja seems to have been a refuge for families from other villages that also suffered a similar fate due to the drought. Kaka wasn't the only one to go and deliver milk daily. There were several lads his age who had come from other drought affected villages to take advantage of their relations' hospitality.

Ba's childhood

According to the passport, Ba was born on 1 January 1930 in Kakabhai Sihan. Ba was also the youngest in her family, having 3 older sisters followed by a brother. The oldest of these sisters, Amritba was married to Kaka's brother, Bapuji. Ba reckoned on being at least 11 years younger than Amritba, so does not remember her marriage as she was only about 2 years old.

Ba's childhood was a difficult one. Even in her 70s, she found it extremely upsetting to talk about it without getting emotional. Her early memories were those of her mother locked up in a room that she would go and give food to after coming back from school. Her mother, my *nani*[18] was deemed to be mentally unstable when Ba was around 4 and was kept in a locked room, taken out in the morning to wash and then kept in isolation. All her sisters were married by this time, so it was Ba who would take her food at mealtimes, clean up the room and tend to all *nani*'s needs. Probing deeper into exactly what her illness was, I'm told she used to slur her speech and was unable to walk properly. Maybe it was multiple sclerosis rather than any mental illness, but it probably wouldn't have mattered anyway. In those days there was no political correctness to worry about. Whilst not quite the law of the jungle, the survival of the fittest was more important than expending undue energy caring for the sick.

---

[17] A long stick balanced on the shoulder with a pail at each end

[18] Maternal grandmother

Kakabhai Sihan with the *otlo* in the middle. *Derasar* is in the background; white building is *apasano*[19] for Jain monks and nuns

Ba remembered her staring out of the window and waving to people. How lonely she must have felt.

I never met my *nani*, but writing about it makes me very emotional and sad. Why did she have to be locked up? Why this punishment of solitary confinement? It wasn't as if she was harming anyone. Ba lived in a joint family with her parents as well as her *kaki*[20]. Her *kaka* had died earlier and so her *kaki* was a widow at a very young age. Ba called her *motiba* rather than *kaki* as a mark of respect as she was her dad's older brother's wife. According to Ba, her *motiba* had a very short temper and also did not get on with my *nani*. So it was probably at her recommendation that *nani* was locked up when her condition started deteriorating. *Nani* wasn't always like this. Ba remembered going with *nani* to visit Ba's *masis* when Ba was around 3 so at this point she must have been fine. I can't understand why my *nana*[21] allowed his wife to be locked up like a caged animal. Why didn't he say something, do something. Ba defended her father saying he had a lot of respect for her *motiba*, and as her husband's younger brother he didn't dare defy her.

Ba was 6 when her mother died. Again Ba was visibly upset that they didn't know the exact time of her death, they just found her dead in the morning. No photo to remember her mother by, Ba was also upset that

---

[19] A resthouse for Jain monks and nuns

[20] Aunt (father's brother's wife)
[21] Maternal grandfather

nani's memory had faded quickly from everyone's minds. Even I didn't know her name, or if I did I'd forgotten so had to ask Ba what *nani*'s name was. She was called Hiraben, ironic really that her name means a diamond, yet she was completely ignored and cast away, her value not appreciated. I wish I could have spoken to my *nana* about her and asked why they locked her up for over 2 years. After her mother died, her father wanted to take *diksha*[22] and become a monk and he went to Palitana with this intention. However some well-meaning relatives managed to coax him back into accepting his responsibilities towards his family.

There are a few villages called Sihan so Ba's village was called Kakabhai Sihan. From some other books written, it appears that of the 52 villages occupied by the Halari *Oshwal*s, this is the oldest village, being about a 1,000 years old. However it was probably occupied by other Gujaratis previously since the history of the Halari *Oshwal*s in Gujarat is only about 500 years old. Sihan was a fertile village as there was lots of water so Ba does not remember any shortages of food. One of their fields was about 3 miles away but the land was very good for crops here. In fact the mud was so smooth and soft here that they often used to put it on their faces. No doubt this is where the idea of mudpacks must have originated. They used to grow millet, peanuts, garlic, onions, and carrots. Being Jains, they would not have consumed the root vegetables but used to grow them as cash crops to sell on. Actually Kaka's family used to eat root vegetables even though they were also Jains. So it depended on how strict you were. Ba's family was very religious and so adhered to a much stricter code of conduct. When Ba got married they used to cook food separately for her as she did not eat any root vegetables. However in time, she managed to change everybody so no one consumed these any more.

Sihan was a privately owned town so 25% of any cash raised had to be paid to the owner of the town. That was the pattern of a lot of villages in those days. If you were lucky and had a benevolent ruler or owner, they would feel it was their duty to look after their people and so in times of difficulty such as famine and drought, these leaders would provide food.

Ba used to go to school probably from the age of around 5. She told me the school was a village community school rather than the government school, free for the girls but the boys had to pay a nominal amount, around 8 *annas* [23] a month, less than a penny.

---

[22] Renounce the world and become a monk or nun

[23] Old indian currency equivalent to 1/16 of a rupee

I asked why it was free for the girls. Otherwise the parents would be reluctant to send the girls to be educated, she replied. I was suitably impressed with the foresight of those who ran the school. The teaching, however, left a lot to be desired. They might have a teacher one month and then no one the next. After a few years the school was taken over by the government.

After coming back from school, Ba would tend to my *nani*'s needs, take her a glass of water, her food, clean and wash the room, wash and dress her and when this was all done, she would go and work in the fields. Her *motiba* was very strict and she was never allowed to play outside with her friends. I can't quite picture Ba as a forlorn little girl who wanted to play outside with her friends. It is an image I need to work on. After my *nani* died, Ba had to give up school and tend to the fields and help with the domestic chores. So at most Ba only had a couple of years schooling.

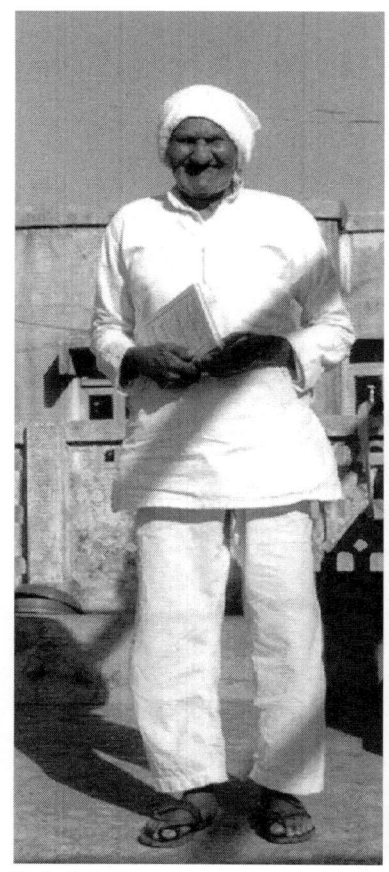

Ba's father   Kaka's father

Amritba, Bapuji, Kaka and Motiba after one of Motiba's fasts

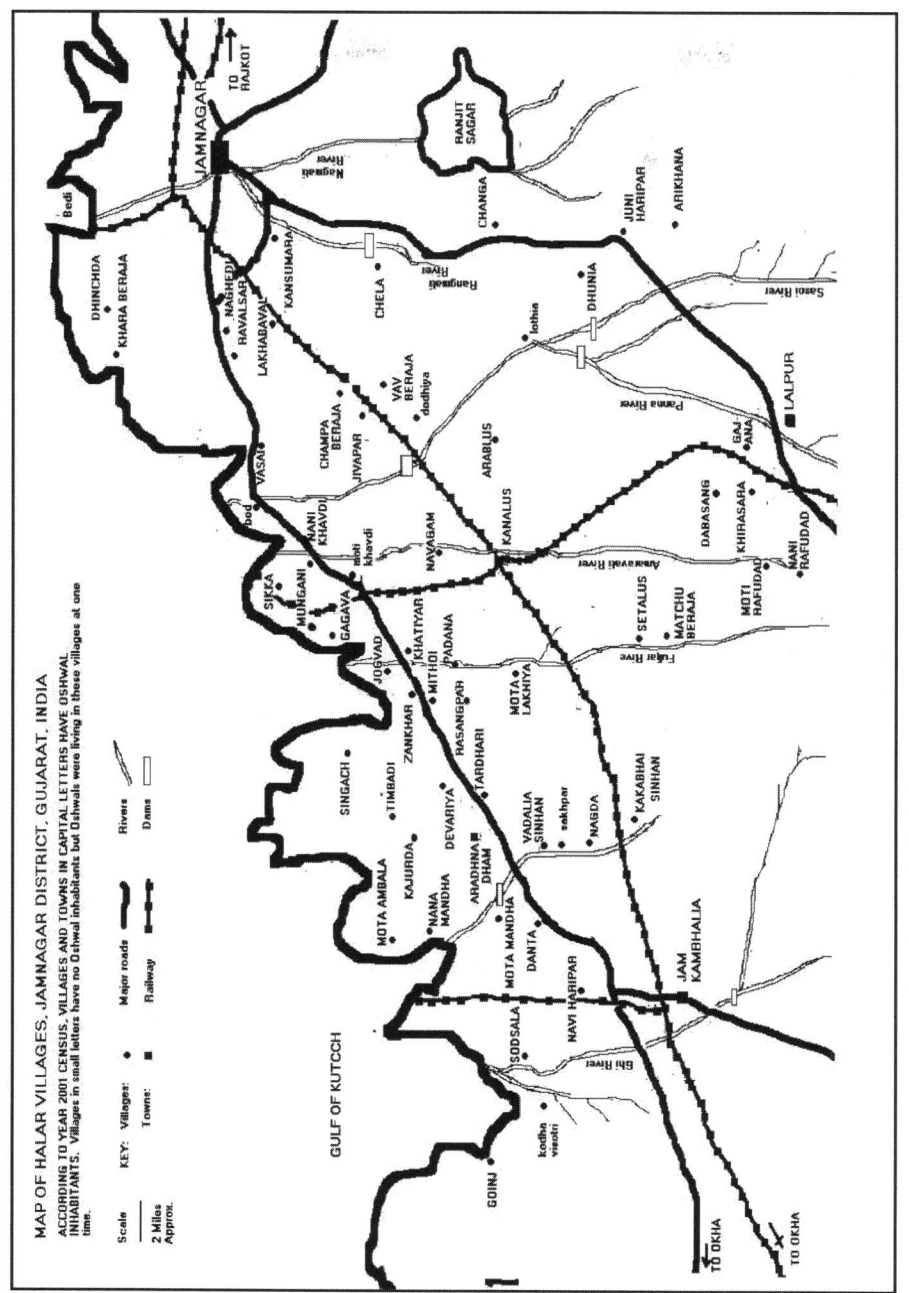

Map showing Kakabhai Sihan and Navagam as well as other Oshwal villages

Kenya

The land of opportunities

In 1941(22 June 1941, according to a piece of paper I found recently in Kaka's writing) at the tender age of 14, Kaka went to Kenya along with his sister-in law, Amritba and young nephew, Zavbhai, to join Bapuji. They left from Khara Beraja and never went back to Navagam.

They went by a steamer boat which ran on coal and took 9 days, much less than the month or so that it had taken for the early settlers who had come in dhows. However this was 1941, the height of the Second World War, and so the boats were prone to attacks from enemy bombs. You were always in fear of your life but it was a risk that they were prepared to take. Kaka related that one day, they had an incident where they heard some cannons going off from another ship but luckily their boat did not get hit.

It was 100 rupees per ticket, (half price for Kaka and Zavbhai) the equivalent of about £2 for all 3 of them, but a princely sum in those days especially for Kaka's family who did not have those kind of savings. So they had to pawn some jewellery to pay for the tickets. You had to pay extra for food so Kaka and party would cook on the ship, having brought their own cooking utensils. A bit like camping I guess. Though camping is a lot more luxurious. On the ship, you brought your own bedding and basically rolled out your bedding on deck or wherever there was space and went to sleep under the stars. Fresh water was only for drinking and cooking so you had to clean yourself with salt water. The ocean tended to be quite rough and ships were not that stable so invariably most people were sea sick a lot of the time. If the sea was particularly rough, you also had to be careful that you did not get thrown overboard as the ship swayed so much from side to side. There was a lot of camaraderie on the ship though. People looked after each other and each other's belongings, they would often cook together and in any case share what food they had cooked.

This trait of food sharing is something that we are fast in danger of losing, perhaps due to embarrassment and trying to fit in and not be different. Kaka and Ba on the other hand would always share whatever food they had with any stranger who happened to be in their vicinity. It's as if it would be rude to eat without passing your food round to others. In 2006 on our way to my nephew Raju's wedding in the States, they were sat in a different part of the aeroplane to the rest of us. Concerned that they were feeling isolated, we tried to swap places with them only to find that they had been giving out their *vadas*[24], *theplas*[25], *ondhwo* [26] to the lady next to them. She said she'd been enjoying all this exotic food and pleaded to let them stay there. They seemed to have broken down any language barriers through this sharing.

The ship would have had this camaraderie that you get with your friends when you go camping. Those that had already settled in Kenya and were going back after a short stay in India, would have told them about the life in Kenya, given them advice and generally helped those like Kaka who were both eagerly awaiting with anticipation but probably a little scared too.

The ship left from a port called Bedi in Gujarat. It would not come all the way to the shore so they had to get on a small boat to go to the steamer. There were a lot of *Oshwal*s on board. Quite a few were visitors from Kenya having already settled there. Upon arriving in Kenya, 5 people who were under 18 were stopped and told they had to go back to India the next day. According to the law, minors under 18 had to be accompanied by a parent or a guardian or return when they were 18. Amongst these was Kaka. The easiest would have been to give up and go back? But go back where? They really did not have anything to go back to and they were all determined to make something of themselves in Kenya.

Kaka was quite indignant that the person selling tickets to them had not made them aware of this issue as the previous ship had encountered the same problem. If they had been made aware earlier, then the passport dates would have been altered to reflect an age of 18. As it was, some of those who genuinely were 18 were showing a younger age on the passport to try and escape paying other taxes.

There were a lot of *Oshwal*s on board who were returning back to Kenya. They knew the system and upon disembarking phoned Nairobi to get hold of various contacts. Some of the young boys who had been stopped with Kaka were particularly well connected and had families who regularly had tea with a councillor called Isher Dass. Isher Dass was alerted that evening of the problem and told that unless he could get permission for the boys to disembark, they would be taken back by ship the next day via Durban. Isher Dass was friends with the immigration officers and managed to organise a month's stay for these 5 on that night.

---

[24] Indian savoury snack
[25] Savoury chapatti
[26] Indian savoury cake

So the boys were allowed to disembark and continue onwards to their destination. Addresses and details had to be provided and after the month was up, the police would come knocking at Bapuji's address in Fort Hall to ask Kaka's whereabouts. Kaka was now an illegal immigrant and he would hide from the police when they came looking for him. After a few months, the councillor, Isher Dass got Kaka's visa and paperwork sorted out and Kaka was now able to officially stay in Kenya.

So how did you get to Fort Hall I asked him? I expected a more detailed and dramatic account of how they had travelled for days on foot but he replied quite simply, by train. By that time the railway line from Mombasa to Nairobi was open for business and so traveling inland was not as difficult as it had been for the early settlers. And then from Nairobi we came to Fort Hall by lorry, he said. So after disembarking, they had reached their destination of Fort Hall in a couple of days, a relatively short space of time.

A station was established here in the 1900s by a man named Francis Hall who had a fort built and hence the name was changed from Mbiri to Fort Hall. Fort Hall was renamed Muranga after we all left Kenya in 1971. However I will continue to use Fort Hall, the name we grew up with. Fort Hall is a town in the province of Muranga in Kenya. It is mainly inhabited by the Kikuyu tribe. Being in the heartland of Kikuyuland, it was Muranga province that gave rise to the Mau Mau movement (an insurgency by Kenyan rebels against the British colonial administration that lasted from 1952 to 1963), and it is seen as the birthplace of the Kenyan independence movement. Fort Hall is located between Nyeri and Thika. The town itself is small but picturesque with an altitude of 4,120 feet above sea level. As I remember, the town had a bank, petrol station, post office, primary school, a gymkhana up by the sports club and a hospital. Around 1950 a *derasar* was built and also around the same time, the old iron sheet *dukas*[27] were demolished and new shops were built with stone and cement. We had to go to the post office to collect our mail, where you had a post box with your name on it. It was a small town with only 2 main streets running across each other, all four sides meeting in the centre, right in front of our shop. Mostly, the living quarters were right behind the shop.

Fort Hall was a small village of around 650 people of which approximately 450 belonged to the *Oshwal* community. The Indians all lived in the town and further up the hill, were the European quarters The Indian community comprised mainly of *Oshwal*s, with a few Patels, Khojas, Singhs. 90% of the town population was *Oshwal*s and most of

---

[27] shops

them were our relatives. The Africans (mostly Kikuyu) stayed outside town in the reserve in their little huts made of clay, dung, branches and dried grass. They grew millet and maize in their *shambas*[28]. Entrance to the huts was very low and one could not enter a hut without bending. Besides the entrance, there was no other ventilation or windows so it was very dark inside.

I wanted Kaka to describe his feelings to me. How did you feel arriving in such a strange environment? Weren't you scared? Didn't you miss your parents? Didn't it feel like a jungle? Kaka was nonchalant. He never gave in to feelings much. There was nothing to be scared about, he was with family after all, his older brother's family and so he accepted his lot and got on with things doing as he was told.

Kaka was told to go to Thika for 5 months to look after one of his cousin's shop. The chance of a possible job opening was never passed up. And so Kaka went to Thika being told it would be a good experience, he could get to learn Swahili and Kikuyu and get some experience in running a shop, quite a change from India where he only knew farming and selling farm produce. Kaka said it was useful experience and he managed to pick some Swahili in the process. That was the pattern in those days. Everyone who came from India would be supported and given work by an elder brother, cousin, uncle until they themselves were able to stand on their own 2 feet and help sponsor other members of their family (be it immediate or extended) to come to Kenya. People were always willing to help and happily share whatever little they had. As Kaka used to say, nowadays, our houses have become bigger but our hearts have grown smaller.

Kaka returned to Fort Hall after 5 months in Thika and started working with Bapuji, who was a partner with one of his cousins. Initially when Bapuji came to Kenya, he had started working for Vidhu Ramji , a family that had been well established in Fort Hall and owned several businesses including a bookshop. He worked there for about 3 years until an opportunity arose for Bapuji to become a partner with his cousin. Kaka's cousin, Zaverchandbhai, (whose father's house, Kaka and the rest of the family had stayed in in Khara Beraja) and Ramjibhai another cousin had a shop in Nairobi which went into liquidation. They also had a shop in Fort Hall, and fearing that the creditors could get hold of assets from the Fort Hall shop, the business name of the Fort Hall shop was changed into Bapuji's name and this is how Bapuji became a partner in

---

[28] Little plots of farming land

that shop from 1939 onwards. So when Kaka arrived Bapuji was already a partner in this shop.

In 1942 Bapuji decided to take on an empty store and turn it into a shop. Behind the store were 2 rooms. These were to be their living quarters. The rent for this was 40 shillings a month, about 50p. All the other villagers were trying to discourage them from renting this shop as they felt that this was not going to be profitable and they would end up in losses. However Bapuji's mind was made up. He dissolved his partnership and received 4,000 shillings, (around £40). He used all this money to buy goods for the shop and started the business in 1942. They both worked extremely hard and the shop was doing well. They looked after their customers so their trade increased through word of mouth. After 12 months, they had made a net profit of 8,000 shillings. This gave them a boost and they continued in this fashion for the next few years.

Coming from a farming background, armed with virtually no capital and little formal education, it is indeed remarkable that Kaka and Bapuji prospered as they did over the coming years. But what they lacked in academic training they made up in hard work and also were willing to seize opportunities through taking calculated risks. In this way they soon became astute businessmen who ran various different businesses. These included shops selling all types of household goods, tailor made clothing, a camera shop, photography, picture framing, dairy, and also being landlords.

Their living quarters were rudimentary to say the least. He told me they initially rented 2 rooms with around 30-40 people sharing the toilet and bathroom. These were not toilets where waste could be flushed away but merely buckets which were emptied by the council daily so they had to tolerate the terrible stench. The housing was not much better either. It was corrugated iron sheets on top and where there were holes, the rain would come through so you had to keep buckets in the rooms to stop getting wet. Also in those days it was very cold especially for them as they were coming from India. So I asked Kaka again whether he ever contemplated going back. No, he was satisfied with how things were progressing. The shop was doing well. Besides, life had been very difficult for them in India.

Those that had had bungalows in India and had still come over to Kenya were not so happy to accept their lot. A lot of them stayed one or 2 years and then went back. This is probably why my grandfather must have gone back when he had come in 1922, 5 years before Kaka was born. For a start it was probably a lot more difficult then. Roads were merely tracks, a lot of the journeys had to be undertaken on foot, and there were few womenfolk so the men had to also cope with all the domestic chores. Also, at that time they were probably not so badly off in India. When my grandfather came to Kenya it is likely that he worked for Meghji Ladha and Co. He was my grandmother's *banevi*[29] and had a big company with a lot of branches all over Kenya. Certainly my grandfather's elder brother worked for Meghji Ladha before he opened up his own shop.

So time passed and the shop began prospering. Before he knew it Kaka had already been here 5 years and now he'd had a letter from his parents telling him that he needed to go back to India to get married. So you didn't have any say in that matter, I asked him, aware that that was the custom in those days. Whatever your parents asked, you did without questioning why. He replied that there was not a lot to discuss, he accepted that this was his destiny. He was going to be marrying his brother's wife's sister, so he probably vaguely knew her. Most would not have seen their wife until the day of the wedding. So I asked him whether he was happier about this or not. Again he showed no emotions. There was nothing to like or dislike. It's not like I could interview her, he replied. There was no occasion to talk and discuss anything, it was accepted that your parents and elders knew what was best for you!

Marriage and all that

Kaka went back to India in 1946 again by a steamer boat, to get married on 21 March 1946. He was 18. Ba was 16. Kaka was always reticent as to how this match was arranged.

As he said they knew the family because Ba's sister, Amritba was his *bhabhi*[30] and other relations advised that this match was indeed arranged by her. Apparently Amritba was impressed with Kaka's kind, calm and peaceful nature and the fact that he easily bonded with kids. She decided he would make a suitable husband for her younger sister and arranged the match despite the height issues.

Marriage was a simple affair in those days unlike the lavish celebrations of today. For a start there still wasn't that much money and although by now they were doing reasonably well in Kenya, it would have been frivolous to spend this hard earned money on an extravagant celebration. Still Kaka reckoned there were around 100 people at the wedding. The

---

[29] Sister's husband

[30] Brother's wife

jaan[31] came from Jamnagar to Sihan, Ba's village in a *khataru*[32]. The wedding took place at night and the *jaan* would have stayed overnight. So there were a few celebratory meals. According to Ba the wedding party had to be restricted to 100. Due to the post war rationing, there was a fine to pay if there were more than 100 guests. Kaka was not aware of this.

So after the wedding, it was a long honeymoon! They stayed in Jamnagar for about 6 months and Kaka didn't do much. They stayed with his parents, Motiba and *motabapa*[33], who had moved to Jamnagar after Kaka left for Kenya from Khara Beraja. Here they had 11 buffalos and a cow and used to sell the milk to earn a living.

Why did you stay so long I asked? Weren't you required in Kenya? There were a few reasons for the delay. It took a long time to get a passport issued for Ba, and when it finally came she complained that it had the wrong name.

She was called Gunvanti by her family but in her passport for some reason they had written Gomi. She must have been initially called Gomi at birth. The other reason for the delay in the trip back to Kenya was that one of Kaka's cousins got married in Jamnagar and used their house as the base for the wedding. So Kaka delayed going back to attend this wedding. For Ba it was difficult to adjust to life after marriage. She had been used to doing housework and farming, but she had never milked cows or buffalos before. She couldn't quite get the knack for this; also she had to learn how to grind flour using a *ghanti*[34]. No sympathies from her mother in law! As a 16 year old she must have wondered what she got herself into! She probably yearned for her beloved Sihan, the village that she was born and raised in.

---

[31] Groom's wedding party
[32] Open topped truck
[33] Paternal grandfather

[34] A hand mill made of stone for grinding flour

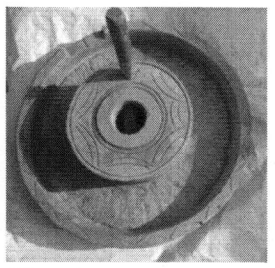

Ghanti

Ba had no say in the matter, nor for that matter did Kaka. But for the woman who arrived as a wife, it was doubly difficult. She was uprooted from her family, to fulfil her marriage obligations and duties of motherhood, and had to follow her husband wherever he went, in this case to Kenya. Except for a small amount of wealth in the form of jewellery she brought with her, she was totally dependent on Kaka for her survival.

Back to Kenya

So in 1946, around 6 months after getting married, both Kaka and Ba came back to Kenya. This time the boat left from Mumbai. Bedi was closed and so Kaka and Ba had to take a train to Mumbai and then board the ship. From Mumbai the ship went on to Cochin.

These steamer ships ran on coal and this ship had run out of coal. It took 3 days to get to Cochin. Once there, coal was loaded onto the ship and this activity took 5 days. While they were docked there, they were allowed off the boat. They had made some acquaintances on the boat and one of these had some relations in Cochin. Along with Ba and Kaka there were some other couples, who all ended up being taken to the relations' house for lunch, and dinner and these relations also took them out and showed them around Cochin. Ba was upset that they never swapped addresses. The people were so hospitable and they had a wonderful time taking in the sights and being looked after by this lovely family who they did not know and were unlikely to ever meet again. Every evening they would come back on the boat and sleep there and then would again go out for the day. They had to come back on the boat at a certain time in the evening in case the ship was ready to set sail again. So this was the pleasant part of the trip, a real holiday, almost like a cruise!

After 5 days the ship set sail again. The ocean was particularly rough and Ba was sea sick the whole time, spending virtually all the time lying down and trying to sleep as any motion would set her off again. She was not sure whether she would be able to make it safely to Mombasa but others, including Kaka's cousin's son Somchandbhai and his wife Shantabhabhi who had married at the same time and were travelling together looked after her and reassured her. This time it took longer, around 10 days so in total they had been at sea for around 18 days, including the 5 days spent in Cochin.

Finally they docked in Mombasa. Unfortunately Ba was in no fit state to take in her new surroundings, the sights and smells of this busy exotic port, the gateway to Kenya and her new life. From other accounts, it appears that the old port of Mombasa was a big square and it was here that one came to welcome and greet those recently arrived and if they did not have anywhere to go or anyone to go to, there would generally be someone from their community willing to take them home. So there were very few who would have been totally lonely in a strange and distant land.

In the early days before the First World War, Mombasa was more like a town in India, with Indian law in place and the usage of Indian currency (Rupees) and Indian postal stamps, however this had changed by 1946 when Ba and Kaka landed. The rupees were changed to shillings in 1922. By 1946, the *Oshwal* community in Kenya had amassed considerable wealth and had already started spending on philanthropic projects in India and Kenya. So when Ba and Kaka arrived there was an *Oshwal dharamshala*[35] in Mombasa for anyone arriving from India who had nowhere else to go. Ba and Kaka however had relations in Mombasa and stayed with them overnight before undertaking the journey to Fort Hall.

So they arrived back in Fort Hall, the 2 brothers working together in the shop and the 2 families all living together behind the shop in 2 rented rooms. They lived in a tin city where the majority of the houses were made from corrugated metal, on wooden floors up on pillars so that the rain water would run underneath. All the *dukas* were built in a uniform design, with metal sheet walls and roofs and wooden floors. Each building had several sections, each consisting of a shop in front and another room behind where the family lived and the cooking was done.

---

[35] Religious resthouse

Photo of Kaka's cousin, Narshibhai and his shop selling all sorts of goods

There were no modern comforts, no electricity, tap water nor indoor flushing toilets. For lighting, they used kerosene lanterns in the shop as well as in the house.

For toilets they had a bucket, and the municipality would send carts around to empty the buckets daily. The door for picking up the bucket was located outside. Niru still remembers that once she was in the toilet when someone came to empty the bucket!

As for water, they would have to go to the bottom of the town where there was a municipal tap and fill the buckets from there. By this time they were doing reasonably well and able to employ servants to bring buckets of water. Water had to be used sparingly though and in those days you showered maybe once or at most twice a week. The toilets and bathroom were in a block and these facilities were shared with around 30-40 people. Ba found it really hard to get used to the foul smell. In Sihan and Navagam, they would have gone to the open fields where there would be an area allocated for attending to your daily needs. This would then have been recycled and used as manure.

Though they were transplanted in Kenya, they still looked to India for their cultural heritage and inspiration. They stuck to their own communities generally and ensured they celebrated all religious and cultural festivals as they would have done in India.

Although *Oshwal*s were peasant farmers in India, their *banya*[36] heritage was strong so entry into business was not perceived as a break from tradition. Indeed Kaka's father had ventured into business in Mumbai when Kaka was small so Bapuji had a bit more experience. I asked Kaka what kind of shop they had. A general store, he replied, selling anything and everything. If they perceived there to be a demand for something,

---

[36] business

they would try and procure it and sell at a profit. Most of their clients were local Africans, not Europeans. There was a power station nearby, near Maragua around 7 miles away, which employed lots of people, so these people would come to Fort Hall to buy provisions.

The shop used to sell clothes, shirts, shorts, all sorts of material, readymade sheets worn by the African women to tie their baby with when carrying the baby around, jaggery, shoes, cigarettes, soap, matches. Bapuji would cut the materials for the readymade outfits which were then stitched by the employed tailor who used to sit in the shop with his manual foot pedalled sewing machine. Everyone who was old enough would help out with the sewing of buttons and hems in the evenings.

Jaggery was used a lot more than sugar as it was lot cheaper. There was a lot of demand for it as the Africans used to make a local brew out of this. Due to the high demand for jaggery, from 1946, there was a control on the price of this so you had to agree the selling price beforehand with the government. There were many traders who had taken advantage of the high demand and had been selling jaggery at an exorbitant price, but they were taken to court, lost and had to pay huge fines. As a result there were fewer traders in jaggery.

Kaka and Bapuji managed to get a supplier from Tanganyika (now Tanzania). Armed with an invoice from him, they went to the government who fixed the price they could sell jaggery at to 40 cents per pound. They purchased the first batch from this supplier but afterwards were free to buy it from anyone else if cheaper as the price they could sell it at was fixed. Being the main suppliers in Fort Hall, they had a monopoly of the market and were able to make good profits out of this, especially as they insisted that customers could not just buy jaggery on its own, they also had to purchase something else. Effective sales technique! This gave Zavbhai who had joined the family business by now, the nickname "Jaggery" amongst the Indian community and Africans.

They also supplied fruits to businesses and traders in Nairobi. Kaka and Bapuji would buy the fruits, mangoes, oranges, or whichever seasonal fruit was available from the local farms. All the children would be enlisted to help sort out the fruit, discard bad ones in a pile to be re-checked by the women later on. Eventually we bought a box body truck to transport the fruits to Nairobi. Even then, we hardly ever went on trips to the countryside. Only occasionally, during the school holidays would we visit relatives in Nairobi or Mombasa.

Other raw materials and goods were obtained from Nairobi as and when required. Usually Kaka would make the trip, in a taxi sometimes staying overnight there with relations. The 2 brothers were both fairly conservative in their outlook and did not take huge risks. The business was successful and growing modestly and they were very careful with their expenses. They did not indulge in frivolous expenses. Their Jain background taught them to be satisfied with their lot and of course they had experienced first-hand being poor and hungry, so they were always wary of undertaking huge gambles or unnecessary spending in case they got caught up in this spiral again.

Their success also coincided with a period of expanding opportunities and high profits generated by World War II, the Mau Mau movement and the booming economy after independence.

After dealing with customers during the day, the evenings were spent in front of the closed shop where all the males would gather. They would cover the floor in front of the shop with a big cloth like a bedspread and all the interested males would sit down for a game of cards. They would normally play *chokadi*[37] or *chhakadi*[38]. This would last for 3-4 hours every night and then everyone went home to rest and sleep.

Rather than quilts, we had thick handmade mattresses. Bapuji would let the tailor make the cover, and fill it up with cotton till it was bursting at the seams. Cotton was grown locally, so we would buy the cotton, sort it out by taking the cotton seed out if there were any left and then leave it out in the sun to be dried for a day or two. Although the cotton bought was already dry, it was left in the sun for a further couple of days in case it had not dried properly.

Then, Bapuji would take a big long needle and with thread as thick as a rope, he would systematically stitch through the mattress so the cotton would not move too much. Though not educated, Bapuji was practical and had a lot of common sense.

Kaka formed a *carom*[39] club with three of his friends. On Sundays, they would all gather and play *carom*. He also intermingled socially and joined the local *bhajan* group with one of the Hindu Punjabi. Even in England, he still enjoyed playing *carom*, as well as cards and loved having us all round for *bhajans*.

---

[37] Indian card game with 4 players
[38] Indian card game with 6 players

[39] Indian board game like mini snooker

After the day's hard work, Kaka would be very tired. Occasionally, his back needed massaging from the pain. He would lie on his stomach and ask one of the children to gently walk on his back. This would last for about 30 minutes and he would say the back felt much better. A good old fashioned massage.

I expected both Kaka and Bapuji to be total saints; not indulging in any smoking or drinking. However on our trip to Turkey he told me that he occasionally used to smoke as did Bapuji. Also unlike strict Jains, they used to eat root vegetables including onions and garlic.

I was shocked since smoking is so taboo now, however in those days a lot more people smoked. He said he first started at around age 10 or 11 when he would light up for his dad and take a few puffs. However Kaka said that unlike his dad, his was never an addiction. He never smoked regularly, only indulging in the habit say once a month or so and gave it up totally in 1951.

In terms of temperament Bapuji and Kaka were quite different. Bapuji was very strict and did not tolerate fools gladly; Kaka, on the other hand, never raised his voice, and was very calm. All my cousins would run to Kaka if Bapuji got mad with them. So it is quite remarkable that the 2 brothers survived so long together in their business.

However they complemented each other. Bapuji though strict was extremely principled. And Kaka as the younger brother always respected his older brother and never went against his wishes.

In August 1947, my oldest sister Niru was born; the housing was still the same, just the 2 rooms and Bapuji's family had also expanded to 4 children with a 5th on the way shortly. So it must have been really cramped.

By the early 50's they had electricity and running water, so no need for kerosene lamps or pails of water. But there was still no hot water from the taps. Any hot water for bathing was boiled on the *sagadis*[40] and later around 1953/54, in a contraption called a *bambo*[41], which continued to be used until we left Kenya.

---

[40] Open stove
[41] A hot water boiling tank

The *bambo* has an inner circular cylinder where the wood/charcoal would be inserted. There is a bigger outer casing which is the main part to hold the water. A tap was attached at the base of circular unit followed by a stand with a tray where the burned charcoal dust will accumulate. When the water was heated in the *bambo*, we would open the tap and fill a bucket with hot water adding some cold water as necessary. This one bucket had to suffice for the adults; as children we had to share a bucket between at least 2 of us.

Bambo   *sagadi*

Bricks and mortar

Over time in Kenya they managed to build a close knit community and had regular social gatherings, relations to visit and weddings to attend. Socialising was always with the Gujarati and predominantly *Oshwal* community. They did not need to interact with the local Africans or the British rulers and by mixing with their own community they were preserving a bit of India in a far and distant land. Some of the big businessmen would have had a wider social circles and fraternised with government officials, however Kaka and Bapuji were not in that league.

Kaka and Bapuji were beginning to savour the fruits of their labour; they were happy to work hard to accumulate some savings for their growing family, but at the same time, playing by the rules and not taking unnecessary risks. To run the shop, you were required to get a government license on an annual basis and all men over 18 had to pay a type of poll tax. The ladies were exempt from this tax.

Around 1952, the government was giving a one year lease for building brick built houses. The land would still belong to the government, but the expenses for the construction would have to be undertaken by the occupants. The government reassured families that after the first year, the leases would be renewed, however some people were a little sceptical. It was a big risk they were taking; if the government went back on its word, and did not renew the lease after the first year, they could lose a lot of money.

However for Kaka and Bapuji, Fort Hall had become their home. The business was doing reasonably well, they could afford to build a house and therefore there was no question of uprooting yet again to start all over. So they decided to take on that risk. They first agreed on a small house. The plot of land was twice the size but they agreed to share this with one of Kaka's cousins. The construction of the house cost them 30,000 shillings. They built a shop with 2 stores at the back for storing goods, 2 bedrooms, a kitchen, a toilet and a shower, with a small courtyard in the middle. This was the house we all grew up in.

Most of the houses were built around the 2 main streets, one going up and the other across, both crossing at the only roundabout, which could be called the centre of the village. There was a big tree in the middle of the roundabout called the Memorial Tree. This tree was there in 1901 when Fort Hall was started. Our house was located on the street going up to the roundabout, the 3rd house down from the top of the roundabout.

At the top of the roundabout, on the corner was a huge house belonging to a man called Chaggan Ghela. Bapuji heard that he intended to sell his house, since he was suspicious of the government's intentions regarding the renewal of the lease. The smaller house was not going to be adequate for all of us so Bapuji thought they should buy this house and build it. The plot of the land on which the house stood was huge and would build 2 large houses, each double the size of the first house agreed. The government, however, were not willing to give all the land to us as they said we already had land for the smaller house. Kaka and Bapuji tried to get their cousin to take all the land for the smaller house and build a bigger house for himself and so we could have 2 houses next to each other on the large plot of land. However the cousin was more interested in the larger plot as well which Bapuji would not agree to part with. So they bought half the house for 15,000 shillings, basically the iron and doors as the land was still owned by the government; they subsequently demolished all this, sold all the iron and managed to make a profit of about 2,000 shillings from these sales! Very enterprising!

So we ended up having a large house at the top of the street, with someone else building a house in between and then a smaller house next to that. This larger house was really large. It had 4 large bedrooms, 2 huge shops , 2 large stores, 2 toilets, 2 bathrooms, a few store rooms, 2 kitchens, and big open air store room for keeping fruit and vegetables. All this was built around a magnificent courtyard where the children used to play games such as badminton. There were a few side entrances and by closing one of these doors, they had 2 other small shops both of which they rented out. This house cost 55,000 shillings to build and was finished around 1954. My cousins and Amritba and Bapuji lived here.

Both of these houses were paid for in cash. Their hard work and thriftiness had finally paid off and now they had made it. So the brothers decided it was time for their parents to join them from Jamnagar. They had been sending money as and when required, but now that they had decent living conditions and their parents were getting on in age, the time was right. Bapuji and Amritba went to India for a few months to wind up everything there. Whilst there, Bapuji sold the house in Navagam as well as the plots of agricultural land and also the house in Jamnagar. All ties with India and Navagam were finally severed and now they had only one place they could call home, Fort Hall.

Our shop on the corner and the large house at the back

Milking money

Around the time that my grandparents arrived in Fort Hall, the brothers expanded into the diary business. This happened by chance but Kaka and Bapuji seized the opportunity presented to them. As our shop was on the corner of the roundabout, basically the centre point of the village, it was in a prime position. So a white farmer used to get milk from his farm in a lorry, park the lorry in front of our shop and sell milk to the villagers from the back of the lorry. As a goodwill gesture, with no commission or any expectation of remuneration, Kaka and Bapuji would mention to our customers that they could purchase their milk from him and so his customer base began to expand quite rapidly. Grateful for this gesture, and unable to cope with the farm as well as this selling, he asked Kaka and Bapuji if they were interested in buying this milk business from him for around 10,000 shillings. For this he would give us the lorry and continue to supply milk to us.

Kaka and Bapuji agreed and employed a driver to pick up the milk from the farm which was about 2-3 miles away. Sometimes my eldest cousin Zavbhai would drive the truck. Demand for milk was constantly increasing and all the milk procured was sold instantly.

The farmer could not supply enough to satisfy everyone's needs and so asked for a loan to purchase some more cows. Kaka and Bapuji then gave him a loan of 10,000 shillings to buy some more cows. Even so the demand kept increasing, so they managed to contact other farms and procured the milk from these farms as well. As a result, they also started supplying other nearby villages such as Saba Saba and Maragua.

On Sunday afternoons, we, the children, would be taken to visit the farm that we were purchasing the milk from. The white farmer looked forward to our visits as his kids were away in boarding schools. The farm was lined with grapefruit trees on both sides of the tarmac road. They would let us cut fruits and we used to pick grapefruits thinking they were huge oranges.

We would peel them, eat a slice or two and then throw the rest away, not understanding why anyone would want to eat these as they were so bitter. The farm also had avocados, but we did not know what they were or what to do with them. The European couple also had a lion cub that you were allowed to pet. I'm not sure any of us dared to!

In the early days, the milk was not stored in a cold compartment but sold within a few hours of the cows being milked. The milk business even kept the ladies busy. Ba mentioned that she normally woke up around 5.00 a.m. to take care of the milk delivery. We had servants who would wash the big 10 gallon empty milk containers after making the deliveries. Whatever milk was not sold had to be boiled immediately. The ladies would boil this left over milk in huge pots. Due to the lack of refrigeration, once the milk was cooled, it had to be further processed to make *pendas*[42] which we sold to other Indians. We even made our own *ghee*[43] from the cream of the milk. The thick coating, formed when the milk was boiled, would be removed and put in a pot to be whisked to separate the whey. Once the whey was removed, the thick cream would be boiled to separate the *ghee*.

As this business grew, we had a big cold water fridge custom made to preserve any excess milk that could then be stored and sold the next day. It was around 8ft by 4ft and had cold water at the bottom. This water was kept cold by electricity and any extra milk containers were placed in this cold water.

Initially the milk was sold by gallons and pints and people would come and bring their containers and get them filled up. However later the store where the fridge was kept was also used as a bottling plant. The bottled milk was mostly bought by the Europeans; as it cost 5 cents more, the Indians were content with filling up their containers.

The brothers had a monopoly on supplying milk to Fort Hall and the nearby villages and other traders wanted a share of this lucrative business.

Someone started getting his supplies from Nairobi and selling the milk at a lower price. We had to respond and lower our prices. We lost quite a few customers who decided to go with the other supplier. However within a month of him starting the business, there were problems. His supplies were not regular, sometimes arriving in the afternoon and quite frequently as a result of this, the milk would go off. Our milk was being delivered regularly and early in the morning, so slowly customers started returning back to us. The competition lasted for about 12 months and in the end he gave up having lost something like 10,000 shillings. As for Kaka and Bapuji, they recovered their customer base but at a cost. The competition had forced them to cut their prices and there were no profits during this period.

---

[42] Indian sweet made from milk and sugar
[43] Clarified butter

Milk - bottling and large containers

Whilst they had survived this threat, around 1960, there were yet more people conspiring to compete against them. Bapuji found out that 4 *Oshwal*s including a cousin of theirs were intending to set up a proper dairy with all the machinery required for pasteurising milk and cold storage in a house that they had bought. The brothers decided that they would not be able to compete against this; even if their customers stayed loyal, the health officials were unlikely to grant them a licence and would require them to have the same standards. The village was not big enough to sustain 2 dairies. So it was decided to try and talk with the consortium, particularly the cousin, to see if they could become a partner in this.

By this time one of the partners had dropped out (he already owned a dairy in Thika) and so the others agreed. They needed the additional funding and also could do with the expertise. My cousin Zavbhai became the manager of this dairy and it was running very successfully.

A little later Kaka and Bapuji found out that the other partners along with the owner of the Thika dairy had bought a dairy in Nyeri without consulting them. So there was a bit of tension between the partners but within 2 years of buying the Nyeri dairy, some of the partners wanted out. The dairy had been losing money, whereas the Fort Hall dairy was making profits. Kaka and Bapuji bought out 2 of the partners of both the dairies and therefore owned 50% of the dairies; the other half was owned by a cousin of theirs along with his partner.

This lucrative milk business continued for some years even after independence but eventually they were coerced into selling the dairies to the African society, who threatened to build one if we didn't sell. Kaka and Bapuji were not interested in getting involved in a long competitive battle; the government and officials would have favoured the African society and it was likely that we would end up making losses. Therefore in 1966 the dairies were sold; the handover of the Fort Hall dairy took place on the same day that Kaka's father died. Kaka said that they started the milk business when his father came to Kenya and ended it when he died. As it was a forced sale, they did not receive any goodwill, however the Society bought all the machinery and retained Zavbhai for his expertise.

A life of leisure for the ladies!

So the businesses were doing well, they had servants to help around the house, the ladies didn't have to go out to work. A life of leisure for the ladies! Wishful thinking! For those of us who think we have it hard, let's look at a typical day in Ba's life in Kenya in the 50's and 60's.

Ba would get up at around 5 in the morning. In the early days she would not have showered daily since it was difficult to fetch water from the village tap, but by the time I was born they had taps at home, so we all took daily showers. Not exactly showers, but we filled a pail of water and then using a jug threw this water on us. Very tiny babies and toddlers would be given a kind of bath by dunking them in the pail of water! Brushing your teeth was a ritual in itself. We never had toothbrushes or toothpaste but instead Kaka would get these special fresh sticks called *dattan*[44]. One end of this would be chewed on until we could make a brush out of it, then we would brush our teeth with this. Once finished, we would split the *dattan* stick in half to make it a tongue cleaner and clean our tongues. Totally biodegradable! Whilst brushing we would go for a walk in our pyjamas to the hill at the top of Fort Hall and there walk barefoot in the grass to improve your eyesight. This obviously didn't work! The whole brushing ritual would take 30-40 minutes but it was an experience that I really enjoyed and looked forward to.

Ba would not come but instead brush at home and get ready quickly so as to start preparing our breakfast after her morning prayers.For breakfast it would be fresh *parathas*[45] or *thepla* on most days. No one had heard of cereals then and bread was a luxury that we got once a month if we were lucky. At this time none of the houses had a fridge, everything was perishable and had to be consumed within a short space of time. All meals were cooked fresh from raw ingredients and there was no question of buying anything readymade. Everything had to be made at

---

[44] Twig used for brushing teeth – in Kenya we used the twigs from acacia trees
[45] Fried chapattis

home. We always had lots of cakes, biscuits, *chevdo*[46], *sev*[47] all freshly prepared at home which we would also have for breakfast.

Even in England, Ba continued with this tradition and made all biscuits, cakes and *nasto*[48] at home till her death.

After breakfast, she would need to clear all the dishes. No dishwashers so if she had a servant their task would be to wash all the dishes. I say if she had a servant as she did not have a regular servant. The wages paid to them were paltry and so there was no loyalty. If they found something better they would not turn up, if they were ill they wouldn't come and if they were required to work in their own *shambas* they would not turn up that day. In return there was no job security, hiring and firing was the order of the day and they would only get paid for the days that they turned up.

So either the servant or Ba would do the dishes and also wash any clothes. The clothes were washed by the beating of the clothes against a stone one after another. The beating would loosen the dirt and scatter the soapy solution away from the clothes, which were then rinsed in clean water in another basin. The clothes would be on the line by 8.00 a.m. so the sun and wind could dry them. Once dried, the clothes needed to be ironed. Initially the iron used was a brass one, imported from India, which was heated by charcoal burning inside.

After breakfast, Ba would start preparations for lunch. Usually this also entailed grinding the millet flour for *rotlo*- there was an electric mill by the river that ground wheat flour but millet had to be ground at home. For lunch everyone would come home so it would be a full Gujarati lunch, entailing *rotli*[49] *saak*[50] salad, *chaas*, *papad*[51], *daal*[52] *bhat* [53]*rotlo*. Whenever there was the mango season, Ba would also make fresh mango juice. Other times we would have fresh passion fruit juice, fresh orange juice, fresh pineapple juice – my mouth is starting to water already at the thought! All these juices had to pressed by hand; mango juice was prepared by straining the ripe peeled mangoes against a muslin or canvas cloth atop a saucepan.

---

[46] Fried indian savoury snack
[47] Fried indian savoury snack
[48] Generic name for all snacks

[49] Chapatti
[50] Curry
[51] Poppadums
[52] Lentil soup
[53] Rice

Shopping for fruit and vegetables was the easiest part as the ladies did not have to go the market or any shops. Some were grown at home, others came from the farms that supplied the milk and some were bought from the African women who went from home to home to sell their home grown produce. After much haggling, a price would be agreed and the best produce selected. I felt sorry for these African ladies who would often be carrying a child on their back and a basket of produce on their head.

After lunch, dishes again and then ready for the next meal preparations. All the rooms, including the bathroom and toilet would need to be cleaned daily so this would be undertaken when there was spare time.

When we came back from school there was always fresh fruit, cakes, biscuits, and *nasto*. If there was time in the afternoon, Ba would make *nasto* or cakes or biscuits. The evening meal would be something simple like *ondhwo* or *dhokra*[54] but still take a couple of hours.

In those days there was no gas cooker or oven so the cooking was done on a little stove fired with charcoal. Yes barbecues every day! We certainly had the weather for it! The meals were cooked using the *sagadi*. Ba even made the *sagadis*. She would take a square tin and have it cut about 10 inches high. Then she had a small window cut at the bottom side and have a door put there so she could open and close this. She would cement the inside making sure all four sides were properly cemented and then make a hump at the top four corners to ensure the pots could sit safely on the top. At the time of cementing, she would also place metal rods (pre-cut by Africans) halfway up in the inner part from side to side making a grill. This would be evenly spaced out leaving a gap of about ¼ inch in-between so when the charcoal is placed on top of these rods, the ash would drop on the bottom part which could be cleaned by opening the little door and scooping it up. The door would also be opened and fanned when too much ash accumulated on the charcoal so the food could cook faster.

After the evening meal, the dishes would be cleared and then once all this was done, there was more work to be done. Usually some buttons or buttonholes that needed sewing with regards to the clothes that they were selling. In fact first and foremost, they had to support the business. Ba told me that sometimes they were called urgently to do some sewing in which case *rotlis* or any other task had to be abandoned. It was of paramount importance that they did not lose any potential sales.

---

[54] Indian savoury snack

So there really was very little time for relaxation. By the time their work was finished it would be around 11pm or even later and they would be exhausted.

However I do recall the odd occasion when other ladies would come and visit and have a social chat. Usually this would be late afternoon around 3 or 4 pm. They might have dropped in to borrow something and then stayed a little longer for a chat. These occasions would be useful in catching up on the latest gossip and moaning about common problems. Also at these times, the ladies would take the opportunity to indulge in the habit of sniffing snuff. Even Ba used to take snuff and my children are shocked that their *Nani* used to take drugs! However it was not so much an addiction, but more a social habit. The container with the snuff would be carried in their blouse pocket and then passed around to whoever was present at the time. It probably helped them relax and unwind after a hectic morning and lunch, but it was nonetheless a filthy habit. I'm not sure when Ba gave it up, certainly before we came to the UK.

In some aspects, the 50s and 60s were the golden days. Nobody worried about security. During the day, no one locked any doors. Ladies would come alone and visit each other in the afternoon or early evenings. We would all play together outside, unsupervised without any fear.

Once a month, the Fort Hall primary school showed Hindi film in the evenings. Everyone looked forward to the movie night and even Ba came a few times.

Also in the sixties, a few families in Fort Hall had acquired a television. A black and white television, only one channel but nonetheless a symbol of prosperity and affluence. We had bought one for the big house and I remember that this object was mostly hidden under a white cloth. Whenever we wanted to watch a programme (usually Felix the cat or Bonanza) we had to ask Bapuji to switch it on for us and he would ask if we had completed our homework before letting us watch anything. On the few occasions that there was something really newsworthy to watch, the whole town would be invited. They would gather in the courtyard and this television would be reverently brought out and switched on.

It was fun growing up in a small town as there was a lot of harmony. The Indians all lived together in the town and everyone knew each other. Since all the ladies stayed home, they helped each other out. If someone had *papad* or *nasto* to prepare, a few of the ladies would get together and would help the host or sometimes several ladies would get together, pitch in their ingredients and all complete the *nasto* or *papad* together which they would then share out equally. The ladies would be able to complete their cooking having a catch up and gossip at the same time. It was also fun for us kids who were usually enlisted to help. Whenever a wedding or some celebration was taking place all the ladies would come and help with the food preparations for days on end as everything was cooked at home.

Even in the business, everyone helped each other, even though many of the shop owners were selling identical goods and so were in direct competition against each other. If one had a bill to be paid and was short of funds, others would pitch in and lend the money without asking any questions. There was complete trust in those days and your word was as good as your bond.

Fort Hall had a nursery and a primary school. When Niru started school, the medium of instruction was Gujarati. As she learnt to read and write the Gujarati alphabet, she would come home and teach what she had learnt to Ba, whose schooling had been terminated aged around 6. Niru really felt very important teaching Ba. This came in useful when we went to India and Niru was in Kenya and Ba could write to Niru. Ba also wrote to her in England when Niru went there.

At that time in the primary school, all the subjects including reading, writing, arithmetic, history, geography and hygiene were taught in Gujarati. In secondary schools, the subjects were taught in English. Later however, when I started even in the primary school, we were taught in English and I actually learnt to read and write Gujarati at home from Ba.

Zavbhai had a talent for numbers and he used to teach Niru and my cousins the multiplication tables. Every night Niru tells me that they all lined up to recite the multiplication tables to 20 in front of Zavbhai. In arithmetic they had to give the answer immediately when Zavbhai questioned them.

Zavbhai got married in March 1958. In those days, the ladies used to cover their faces with their sarees (*laaj*[55]) when talking to their husbands or other men. I recently saw some photos of Zavbhai's wedding, and his wife Kanchanbhabhi's *laaj* was so long that you cannot even make out who he is marrying!

---

[55] Long veil

Pushpamasi passes away

Ba's sister Pushpamasi and her husband Premchandmasa were living in Mombasa and at the time were leading a comfortable life. During her pregnancy, it appears that she may have swallowed some medication intended for external use and as a result, had a mental breakdown. She came to Fort Hall to stay with Amritba and Ba for about a month to recuperate but it seems she did not recover fully. My *masa*[56] then decided to go back to India.

Following the boat journey to India, one of the benefits of being sea sick was that it apparently helped her recover from the effects of the medication such that mentally, she was feeling much better. The rest of the children were born in India, so she had 5 young children to look after. However in India, they had financial setbacks due to a business partner cheating my *masa*. On top of that *masa's* sister in Mombasa was terminally ill with cancer. In those days men made a lot of decisions without consulting or even informing the wives and Pushpamasi found out from a neighbour that my *masa* was planning to go back to Kenya, with the intention of bringing his sister's children to India to live with them. Worried about looking after and feeding so many young children, when she could barely do this for her own, she once again succumbed to depression and shortly afterwards,burnt herself to death, leaving her young children, the youngest was probably just a year old. It is always difficult to understand why someone would take their own life, but to take it in such a horrific way is beyond comprehension. I find it upsetting. I cannot comprehend how she can have abandoned her innocent children. Was there no one she could turn to? Clearly she felt there was no other alternative. In those days, once a woman was married, she had left her parental home for good. So she probably did not feel she could turn to her father or brother in Sihan. She must have felt so lonely.

Pushpamasi's death had a harrowing effect on Ba and Amritba, but there was little they could do. Both had young families of their own, so they were unable to go to India to help look after the young children. As a result of the financial setback, the family relocated to Lakhabaver where they had a farm and cattle and my *masa* remarried.

Unfortunately the family was to experience more tragedy. Once, years later, after getting fodder for the cattle, *masa* must have been thirsty, and decided to drink from the well. In those days, there was no safety mount for the wells. My cousin Taraben had been with him in getting the fodder

---

[56] Uncle (mother's sister's husband)

but then had come back home whilst *masa* gathered neem twigs for use as *dattan*. A few moments later, they heard faint sounds and upon investigating, found that *masa* had tripped and fallen into the well. Taraben ran to the railway station, the nearest area from where they could ask for help. 3-4 men agreed to come and help and after a lot of struggle they managed to get *masa* out of the well. Although alive, *masa* was poorly, and taken back home to have heat fermentation; a village doctor attended to him. However everyone agreed that *masa* needed to be taken to Jamnagar for treatment. The ambulance arrived much later, around midnight, but unfortunately he died on his way to the hospital.

In due course, all my cousins married, however in a further tragic twist of fate, 2 of them, (Rasila and Khusal) committed suicide and a third cousin, Navin died in a train accident. How can so many tragedies befall one family? I hope that a better fate awaits my cousins that are still alive, Mansukhbhai and Taraben and their families. I recently met Taraben; I have never met Mansukhbhai but hopefully I will one day.

Premchandmasa and Pushpamasi

Ba with Taraben up on the roof at Taraben's flat in Bangalore

Tragedy by the river

24 June 1962 was indelibly printed in Kaka's mind. Till his dying day, he recalled the day vividly much the same as the millions who are still able to recall exactly what they were doing on 22 November 1963, when John F Kennedy was assassinated. For the villagers of Fort Hall, 24 June 1962 was when the heart of that village was ripped open.

It was a beautiful Sunday morning and my cousin Shantu who was 19 had just finished her exams that week. Just 2 weeks earlier, she had said goodbye to her younger brother Gulab who had come to the UK to study for his 'A' levels. The night before she had gone to the airport, this time to bid farewell to the 'three Shashikants' – 3 young men all called Shashikant, 2 of whom were Kaka's cousins' sons. They were also coming to the UK to pursue their studies further. She had written a farewell letter to Gulab and sent it with this trio.

She had gone for further tuition on Sunday morning, and after this, she, along with a few friends, decided to go for a picnic by the river, where the mill (for grinding wheat) was situated. It was a beautiful spot, scenic and tranquil and the girls were keen to unwind and relax after a hectic term. My Amritba was trying to dissuade her not to go as the ladies were making *papad* and could have done with some help. However, Shantu was insistent and wanted to celebrate the end of exams. Some other younger girls also decided to join them so in total around 15 girls went to this picnic spot. Even Bena, who was 8 at the time wanted to go but she would only go if one of my other cousins went and as this cousin did not go, Bena didn't go.

It was about 2 miles away and the girls were in high spirits as they ambled leisurely to their destination. Once there, they sat and chatted by the edge and maybe even played a few games. It was a hot day and the girls were keen to wade in the river and cool down. The younger girls continued to stay by the edge of the river. It is not clear whether the older girls stopped them from crossing the river. The older girls, 6 of them, waded across the river and then climbed on top of a huge stone that lay in the middle of this calm river.

Suddenly they heard the younger girls shouting at them to hurry back to the edge, as there was lots of water coming. By this time, however, the older girls were not sure they would be able to get across to the edge safely, due to the depth of the water. It was a huge stone, very firm and quite high and so they thought their best option was to stay put. It was unlikely that the water would come up that high. Unfortunately the water just kept coming, now with such a force, that the girls got thrown off this huge rock by the force of this water.

The younger girls ran back to the village as fast as they could and explained what had happened. It was Sunday afternoon and the shops were closed. Kaka had been sitting outside someone's petrol station, chatting but he sensed there was something not quite right. He was feeling listless. Upon hearing the girls screaming all the villagers ran to the picnic spot. They saw lots and lots of water. The river, usually calm and still, was now a mighty torrent, the water gushing forth. It was as if someone had opened the cage of a wild animal, and let it loose on an unsuspecting victim.

The villagers could only look on helplessly. The girls were nowhere to be seen apart from one. By the sheer force of the water, this girl had been thrown on to a higher stone and clung at it with dear life. Nobody was able to rescue her. To go into this raging river was risking certain death, and so they kept talking to her to hang on. Other villagers walked down the river edge to see if any more girls were hanging on like this. Alas no. By this time the authorities had been alerted. The river once again became calm and the villagers were able to rescue the frightened girl and comfort her. Scouring the edge of the river, one girl was found within the next few hours; another was found later that night and yet another the next day; my cousin Shantu was found on Tuesday. The last girl was found after a month and her body was so badly decomposed that she couldn't even be brought home for cremation.

What went wrong? There was a dam about 5 miles upstream and although the policy was that it should never be opened during the day, one of the employees did and in the event caused this awful tragedy. Apparently he was drunk. He must have come into work and decided to open the dam as there was lots of water and thought he should release some of it. The dam was about 5-7 miles away and this opening may have caused other tragedies since other people could be washing their clothes on the river or washing themselves however Kaka was not aware of anyone else being affected by this incident. Maybe their story was never told.

I am not sure whether the employee was ever prosecuted and charged with manslaughter. Certainly there was a case and Kaka recalled that all the victims' families received some compensation, a paltry sum of around 8,000 shillings. The families were advised by their lawyers not to pursue this further. In any case, the villagers were too engrossed in their own grief to think about fighting for more compensation. The funds received were used towards the cost of building a swimming pool to ensure that all children learnt how to swim.

In memory of Shantu, Bapuji asked that the names of the children born after her death should start with the letter S. Shailesh was born a few months later, then Sanjay, Zavbhai's son and Samir, Dinuben's son.

Shantu – portrait and one where she is making chapattis

Daughters galore and finally a son

I was just over 2 years old when Shantu died, so have no recollection of the tragic event. According to my other cousin, she had cut my hair very short when I was little, much to the dismay of Amritba and my grandmother.

The last of four girls, my birth was not particularly welcomed. My grandmother is said to have exclaimed 'not another girl' upon hearing about my birth. Although times had changed and dowry systems abolished (at least in the *Oshwal* community) girls were still an unwelcome burden, and the parents were always considered blessed if they had a son. Daughters were after all considered to be someone else's family, since they would eventually marry and live with their in-laws. So they were really considered to be in your hands for safekeeping until the time was right for them to be married off. Boys on the other hand would be there to provide for and look after their parents in their old age. So the more boys you had the more blessed you were considered to be.

Manjula my second sister tells me that she used to tell Kaka off as he would never hold me in his arms when I was a baby. Kaka was very good with kids and she could never understand why he wouldn't hold me. Maybe in some way he might have resented having another girl and this was his way of expressing it.

My brother Shailesh was born in September 1962 – finally a boy! So my mum was forgiven and all was well. I say this because it was always considered to be the woman's fault if she could not bear children and it was also assumed that her body determined the sex of the child. And with everything being attributed to your past deeds, it was as if she must have done something wrong in her previous life if she kept having girls. Certainly she was out of favour with my grandmother not only for this but also because when she got married her culinary skills were lacking. In those days you were judged by whether you knew how to make *rotlo* and Ba didn't know how to make it when she married. Ba had a hard time when she got married and having all these girls didn't help.

Niru the oldest, was born in 1947. As the oldest, she was also the most hard working and had to do all the chores around the house such as cleaning, cooking, sewing and looking after her younger siblings. Ba constantly reminded us of how hard Niru has worked - in fact, even now Niru is unable to relax as she feels she is wasting her time if she is sitting idle.

Manjula was born in 1952 and from all accounts was a bit of a tomboy and also Kaka and Ba's most demanding child. She would throw temper tantrums if she didn't get her way, break her slates (in nursery and early primary school we would have slates rather than exercise books for our work) on a daily basis or lie down on the dirt road and refuse to go to school. She tells me that even all the boys were terrified of her as she would threaten to beat them up if they harassed her or her friends. Manjula would also get into fights with her siblings and Niru still bears the scars of a knife that Manjula threw at her. Actually Manjula wasn't aiming for Niru but rebelling against doing some house chores and in a fit of temper chucked the knife. Still Manjula was the one fighting against injustices. She would speak out when the rest of us didn't dare or didn't care. She insisted on Kaka getting a radio for us when Bapuji got the television for the larger house. And of course being the tomboy that she was, she would be the one climbing up and getting the fruits from the passion fruit and papaya trees that grew by our house.

Bena was born in 1954 and according to Niru, she always used to get out of doing her chores. Niru ended up doing all the work whilst Bena and Manjula were fighting and pulling each other's hair. Bena had to start school a year early, as Manjula whinged about going to school whilst Bena was allowed to stay at home. Bena was always the most fashion conscious of us all, sporting patchwork leather trousers and hot pants as a teenager.

Born in 1960, I was very placid. Always wanting to impress my older sisters, I would pander to all their whims and would end up doing chores set for Bena and Manjula so that they let me join in their activities. Other times I was quite happy to sit in a corner and read. I loved books and would get so absorbed and immersed in them that I was completely unaware of everything else around me.

Bena, me and Manjula

Shailesh my brother was born in 1962 and was the baby and the darling of the family. All of us wanted to sleep next to him when he was a baby as he was so cute and cuddly. He loved sweets and chocolates, a treat that was very rare for us. Whilst I would save mine for weeks on end, he would scoff his in an instant, so I usually ended up giving him half my share as well.

Me and my siblings and some of my cousins

Political uncertainty

From around 1952, the political climate in Kenya had started changing. Mau Mau, the guerrilla movement uprising was an insurgency by the Kenyan rebels against the British colonial administration that lasted from 1952 to 1960. The core of the resistance was formed by the Kikuyu tribe

For several decades prior to the eruption of conflict, the occupation of land by European settlers was an increasingly bitter point of contention. Most of the land appropriated was in the central highlands of Kenya, which had a cool climate compared to the rest of the country and was inhabited primarily by the Kikuyu tribe. By 1948, 1.25 million Kikuyu were restricted to 2000 square miles (5,200 km^2), while 30,000 settlers occupied 12,000 square miles (31,000 km^2). The most desirable agricultural land was almost entirely in the hands of settlers.

As a result of the poor situation in the highlands, thousands of Kikuyu migrated into cities in search of work, contributing to the doubling of Nairobi's population between 1938 and 1952. At the same time, there was a small but growing class of Kikuyu landowners who consolidated Kikuyu lands and forged strong ties with the colonial administration, leading to an economic rift within the Kikuyu. By 1953, almost half of all Kikuyus had no land claims at all. The results were worsening poverty, starvation, unemployment and overpopulation. The economic bifurcation of the Kikuyu set the stage for what was essentially a civil war within the Kikuyu during the Mau Mau Revolt.

The conflict started from about the late 1930s and aggravated in the 40s and 50s due to the lack of acknowledgement of the Kikuyus' grievances by the British government. Around 1952 it was clear that a political solution to the crisis was unlikely and therefore the Mau Mau became more violent, attacking and killing not only white settlers but also any Kikuyu who were perceived to be government collaborators.

They would attack their victims by night and usually hack them to death; there were also reports of loyalists being burnt. Any atrocities committed by the Mau Mau were widely reported in the British press contributing to the notion of the Mau Mau as blood thirsty savages. In turn the British government also became more aggressive and persecuted and killed around 20,000 Kikuyu, even when some of these were not proved to be rebels.

A state of emergency was declared in 1952 and lots of leaders arrested and interned including Jomo Kenyatta who actually had spoken out against the Mau Mau. The emergency lasted until 1960 but by 1956 the British military had gained the initiative as by this time the Mau Mau had run out of ammunition and were low in supplies. However the

British had also granted lots of concessions to appease the Africans including land reform. They were also coming round to the idea of one person one vote – majority rule.

The choice that the authorities in London faced was between an unstable economy which was costing a fortune in military expenses run by settlers who contributed little to the economic growth of the Empire or a stable colony run by Africans that contributed to the coffers of the empire. The latter option was preferred, however it lasted only briefly, since Kenya achieved independence in 1963.

Although they lived in the heart of Kikuyuland, Kaka and Bapuji were not directly affected by the Mau Mau uprising since they were not politically active. They were basically keen to keep a low profile and get on with their business. As a result of the troubles, business was better since there were so many military personnel who had more spending power than the locals.

Nonetheless they were not completely immune to what was going on around them especially as there was talk of businesses only being allowed to operate if they were run by Kenyan citizens. This was to limit the Asian presence in commerce in Kenya since a lot of Asians had opted for a British passport rather than a Kenyan one. Although they were financially secure and had a very comfortable life in Kenya, Kaka and Bapuji still had nagging doubts about life after independence. They were given the choice of opting for British or Kenyan citizenship and decided to opt for a British passport whilst still wishing to remain in Kenya. They were hedging their bets. Although they had not been to Britain, they were aware of how the British ruled and preferred the devil they knew rather than throw in their lot with the volatile and unpredictable Africans. To further hedge their bets, they decided that one brother should move to India and explore business avenues there. So Kaka who had a British passport, a Kenyan business and house, decided to move to India to live and make a life there.

Indiaaaah – my motherland

So on the 14 November 1964, we set sail for India. Niru did not come with us as she was still studying for her matriculation exams and the plan was that she would be coming to London afterwards to study. I was not quite five and don't have much recollection of the journey but it was again by ship from Mombasa.

We landed in Porbander about 10 days later and I promptly got lost. I must have been looking at the scenery or something and not noticed that the rest of them had moved on. Of major concern to my parents was the fact that I was wearing a brand new watch, a present upon leaving Kenya. The worry was not that this fairly expensive watch would get stolen, but that I could get kidnapped as a result of the watch. They need not have worried; a passer-by stopped to find out why I was crying and somehow managed to lead me to them.

We had every intention of settling in India and so had packed all our utensils to take there. In Kenya we had no electric or gas cooker, no fridge, but when we went to India we took these items as well. I can't quite understand why we took these as we never unpacked them and used them. We didn't have our own house in India. A cousin of Kaka's (Raishikaka) had a big bungalow in Jamnagar. He was living in Fort Hall so the house was empty and he asked us to stay there so at least the place was looked after and we didn't have to look for anything else.

The bungalow was absolutely beautiful and luxurious; marble tiles on the floors, seven huge bedrooms, three bathrooms, a dining room and a kitchen. It was in the middle of a large compound with several other houses and most of the families were *Oshwal*s. The compound was really pleasant but as soon as we stepped outside it was a different matter. Manjula says she used to hate going to school early in the mornings as we would have to pass a line of people answering their daily call of nature!

We used to go to an English school called St Anne's Catholic School for girls. I don't remember much about the school but I recall that Manjula and Bena used to have a private tutor at home to teach them Sanskrit and Hindi. I must have also picked up some Hindi as Niru recalls that I used to write letters to her in Hindi.

Kaka was trying his hand at business in Jamnagar and as his first venture bought a large plot of land along with my Veljimama (Ba's brother), and Gulabmasa (Ba's sister, Dahimasi's husband) and Ladhamasa (Ba's cousin's husband). The land belonged to a Muslim who had donated half of the land to his community for use as a cemetery. The other half had been given to a Hindu tenant farmer. According to the laws in India at the time, this farmer would become the owner of the land after renting it for 4 years. The Muslim was not keen on this happening and therefore had asked his solicitor to seek buyers for the land. The farmer would be paid compensation from the proceeds. The sale of the land was agreed at 1.75 rupees per square foot and the total land was 100,000 square feet.

So all parties agreed that 75 *paise*[57] would go to the farmer and 1 rupee per square foot would go to the Muslim community. The sale was agreed and the farmer got paid his share and vacated the land. However all land sales had to be approved by the Jamnagar *Nagar Palika*[58] and he had not been informed of this sale. So he stopped all the paperwork and would not proceed with anything, including deleting the farmer's name from the deeds. The Muslim wanted his money but because the deeds could not be assigned to Kaka and his associates, there was stalemate. This lasted for around 2 years, well after we'd left Jamnagar. In the meantime the land prices were rocketing and so after a few years a real estate guy from India said he would buy the land from them and deal with all the paperwork to make it his and build houses. Kaka and *masas* sold their share but Veljimama was determined to keep his share. Originally Kaka and the others had bought the land to build houses and sell at a profit but Kaka realised how difficult and cumbersome it was to do business in India.

Living in India gave us the opportunity to bond with my Dahimasi's children who also lived in Jamnagar and with my Veljimama's children who still lived in Ba's village Kakabhaisihan. We used to go to Kakabhaisihan fairly regularly to stay there and would end up talking late into the night with our cousins much to the chagrin of our parents and Ba's *motiba* who was also still alive at the time.

Whilst in India Kaka and my Gulabmasa took a trip traveling around India for about a month leaving Ba to look after us. Niru thought Kaka had gone to try his hand at some business venture there but it was just a fun trip. Kaka loved traveling and with Gulabmasa, he had a companion who also enjoyed it. They went to Hyderabad, Indore and a lot of other places. Gulabmasa kept a detailed diary of all the places they'd visited which Ba found after Kaka's death.

---

[57] Indian currency -100 paise in a rupee
[58] Head or mayor of town

Kaka and Gulabmasa

Although the intention had been to settle in India, Kaka realised that it was going to be hard to do business there and we, the children were apparently really missing Kenya. So after about 6 months, Kaka decided to go back to Kenya, taking our passports with him so that he could get them stamped for a return entry back to Kenya; Niru, along with my cousin Ansuya and a couple of other girls were planning to go to England to study and Kaka thought he would also see them off. He had every intention of returning to India and then us all coming back to Kenya together.

But things never happen as planned. Soon after he left, Ba got an electric shock. She was cleaning some utensils in the *chok*[59]. You sat in this little designated area and washed the dishes underneath the tap. Your feet and lower legs would get wet from this washing but they dried soon enough in the heat. As she was washing the dishes, she felt tingling in her legs and feet. Not knowing what was happening she ignored it for a while and carried on. However after a few minutes it kept getting stronger and not realising the severity of the situation, she asked Bena to come and see if she could feel it. Bena got thrown off balance by the strength of the current and my mum realised it was something serious.

---

[59] Square cubicle like a shower base without the upper walls for washing dishes

Washing dishes and clothes in a *chok*

They both got out of there quickly and called somebody from the compound. They confirmed that it was an electric shock due to faulty wiring but luckily she did not sustain permanent damage or paralysis. However for a while Ba couldn't feel her left side at all and even years later she sometimes complained of pain in her leg due to the electric shock.

As if this wasn't enough, a war had started between India and Pakistan. Jamnagar was declared a conflict zone and people were advised to evacuate Jamnagar. The main thrust of the conflict was in Kashmir, however there was an element of aerial conflict as Jamnagar had a military airbase as well as a naval base. As a result of these air raids, which took place mainly at night, a curfew was imposed and those residents that remained in Jamnagar were advised to hide in dig out shelters. Most of the people in our compound had fled Jamnagar returning to their villages or to some relations. Even my Dahimasi's family had left Jamnagar. So Ba was on her own and her *motiba* came to persuade her to come back to Sihan. Ba refused as Manjula and I had yellow fever and Shailesh had measles and the medical facilities as well as food in Sihan would have been problematic. Her *motiba* was not impressed with Ba's obstinate attitude and left; however my *nana* then came to Jamnagar more for moral support rather than any other help, as he was more frightened than the rest of us! Ba didn't make us sleep in the bunkers for fear of us becoming more ill from our existing illnesses, however *Nana* would hide in the dig-out as soon as dusk came. We stayed indoors but were not allowed to switch any lights on for fear of being bombed. Ba told me you could hear the bombings at night and whilst frightened, she had full faith that through her prayers mainly the *Navkar mantra*[60], we would all be safe. And it worked. She always said that this is what saved all of us and would tell everyone about the power of the *Navkar mantra*.

News of this conflict had reached Kenya and Kaka decided it was pointless for him to come back to India but told us to return as soon as possible. There was, however, the small matter of our passports still being in Kenya. Luckily he managed to send these to us via a relative. Ba had to pack things in a hurry. We only took the bare minimum and left everything else in Jamnagar, a sore point for many years as she left most of her prized possessions in India. We finally returned back around October 1965, again by ship. The last few months had been horrendous and so we were finally glad to be coming back home to Kenya. Manjula swore that she would never return back to India!

Home again but a lot of upheaval!

In 1965, we were back again in Kenya after our brief sojourn. The shop was still operating and Kaka was back running the business with Bapuji. Niru had already gone to England. I started primary school. I was a year younger than the rest of the class, because I'd already had schooling in India.

Fort Hall only had a primary school so after the age of 12 we had to go to Nairobi and stay in a boarding school to continue with our education. This is what Niru had done prior to coming to the UK. She had finished her matriculation exams (the equivalent of GCSE's) and then came to England for vocational training to become a secretary. Niru had already come back to Kenya sometime around May 1967, having completed her training. I was overjoyed. 12 years older than me she took me under her wing, and taught me how to speak English properly. She also taught me how to swim. However after only a few weeks, she went to Thika to work there.

In Thika, Niru went to stay with my cousin Zavbhai and worked as a secretary there. By this time Zavbhai was managing the Thika dairy. Some politician had wanted to buy this dairy but the owner had sold it to the African cooperative, the same organisation that had bought our dairy in Fort Hall. In fact Zavbhai had been training the employees at the

---

[60] The most important Jain prayer

society in Fort Hall and as they had bought the Thika dairy, he was asked whether he could also help train those employees. He was warned by some not to go to Thika as the original owner had antagonised the politician by selling it to the cooperative society rather than him and it was always difficult to predict what these politicians would do.

The politician was not too happy about not being consulted on the sale and wanted revenge. So he sent a couple of armed police to arrest the original owner. However they asked who the manager was and although Zavbhai was not the manager, nor the original owner, not knowing what they were after, he replied he was the manager. He was then promptly escorted off the premises, and taken home where they asked for his passport. Kanchanbhabhi asked him why and said she would not give it until she found out why but Zavbhai insisted that she gave it. These were armed police and it was no knowing what they were capable off. He was then taken in an open truck to Embakasi airport (now renamed Jomo Kenyatta) at the back of which was an army camp and he was interned here for 3 days. Not having any telephones in those days, Kanchanbhabhi was helpless and could not alert anyone. However some family friends saw Zavbhai being taken in an open truck and followed the truck which is how they found out where he had been taken.

The African Cooperative Society of Thika was furious when it found out what had happened and they joined forces with the societies of Nyeri and Fort Hall (these dairies had been sold off previously to them) and took a delegation to see President Jomo Kenyatta, affectionately known as Mzee or 'old man'. They pleaded with him to release Zavbhai. They told him Zavbhai had been teaching them how to manage the dairy, how to get better yields of milk, and Zavbhai was not the one who had done anything wrong. Kenyatta was sympathetic but his hands were tied too as his vice president Daniel Arap Moi was behind this so he asked the society to take their case to Moi. Moi was unwilling to listen as it would mean conceding he was wrong. In total 12 people (5 Asians and 7 Europeans) had been interned and were due to deported with some media hype on how they were not good Kenyan citizens so to admit to a mistake on the arrest of one would be embarrassing.

After 3 days in the internment camp, Zavbhai, along with the other 11, was deported to England with literally nothing apart from the clothes he was wearing. The only consolation was he did not have to pay the airfare! Realising the media had got hold of the story and would be trying to question them when they landed in the UK, they decided to split up and blend with the other passengers, so as not attract attention. Upon arrival in England they were housed and provided some pocket money until they were able to survive on their own. Zavbhai had already visited the UK in 1963 and was familiar with the transport system and his younger siblings, Gulab, Ansuya as well as Dinuben and her husband Rasikbanevi were already here, so he just surprised them early the next day!

Kanchanbhabhi joined him a few months later with her 2 young children, Raju, 6 years old and Sanjay, 4 years old. They found it very hard to adjust initially. There was little variety in the fruits and vegetables they could buy, they had to wash their own clothes, wash their own dishes, and clean the house themselves. On top of that it was extremely cold and they had no central heating.

By 1966, Manjula was old enough to go to a boarding school in Nairobi, but she just hated boarding school. She would always complain about everything there and kept saying that she wanted to go to London to study. Every week Kaka would make a trip to Nairobi to see her and bribe her into staying. Eventually, after a year of her constant moaning, in December 1967, he decided to give in and send both Bena and Manjula to England to study, a brave decision considering neither Kaka nor Ba had been here. But there were all our other cousins.

A few months later in February 1968, my cousin Dilip also joined them at the tender age of 12. The decision to send him was taken literally overnight as it became clear that even those with British passports would need visas and therefore find it difficult and time consuming to come to the UK. Lots of people came to the UK at this time and that period is commonly referred to as the exodus. The UK was tightening up its immigration policy and Asian British subjects were to be restricted to 1,500 per year based on a voucher system. When Bapuji found out this was going to happen, he asked Dilip whether he wanted to go the UK to study. Dilip had just come back from a huge Scouts Jamboree weekend. His siblings had sent photos of a green land with horses and immediately he said yes. So the next day he went to the school to advise them that he would no longer be coming there. He barely had time to pack and say goodbye to his friends and teachers as he, along with some other youngsters, was dispatched to the UK within 3 days. There was no time to alert anyone in the UK that he was arriving there. Luckily he was travelling with a cousin who had come on holiday to Kenya from the UK, but being unable to contact his siblings, they had to go to another friend's flat. Here they phoned Zavbhai and managed to convince him that it really was Dilip, this was not a joke, before Zavbhai picked him up! Amritba was totally heartbroken upon parting with the one child that still remained at home. All the rest were in the UK, working or studying.

To console her, I would often go and stay there for weeks and months and read them the letters that my sisters and cousins wrote.

An idyllic childhood

It was 1968 and the political climate was becoming more and more tense. Kaka and Bapuji were not sure how much longer they would still be able to carry on with their business. A lot of businesses had been served with notices to close their shops but fortunately we had escaped this first wave of notices. So it was business as usual until external forces forced us to change. As children we were oblivious to the political situation and loved our environment. We would go to school and come home finish our work and then be out playing with our friends until our parents called us for dinner. No play stations or other computer distractions, we would play in the streets. On the rare occasions that we were allowed to watch TV, we had to go the big house and Bapuji would switch it on for us. None of us were allowed to touch the TV ourselves and when we had finished, he would come and switch it off for us. I particularly enjoyed watching Felix the cat and Bonanza.

Our parents left us to our own devices, happy in the knowledge that the village was safe. It was a small village where everyone knew each other and everyone looked out for one another. We didn't have many toys but invented our own games. One of my favourites was a game called *gilli danda*[61], a kind of cricket game except instead of a ball we had a short wooden rod about 6 inches long that was pointed and sharpened on both ends. We would take a long stick and hit the end of this rod with the stick, hoping it would get airborne, after which we would hit it again as far as we could. The fielders would try and catch this rod whilst the batter would try and score a run. All this was played in the back streets which had an uneven surface and was like a dirt track with lots of stones everywhere. Of course we would get hurt from the games we played but all these would be healed with the application of *zambuk*[62], the panacea for all cuts, grazes and sprains. Even today I apply it to my kids; they always thought it was some kind of Indian herbal medicine but were actually amazed to find out that it was manufactured in the UK.

---

[61] Outdoor game played with a short rod and a long stick
[62] Medicated ointment

Dilip, Raju (Zavbhai's son) and Shailesh

Me in front and Sanjay sitting behind

When we came back from school we would eat lots of fruit; sugarcane if that was in season, which we would first peel, then bite off into small pieces and then chew, all with our teeth, including the peeling of the skin! It was probably this that made our teeth really strong; I had no cause for visiting a dentist in all my time in Kenya. We rarely had chocolates, crisps or fizzy drinks. We looked forward to these treats when we went to Nairobi to one of our distant *mama's*[63] (Zavumama) house; he owned a shop which served *bhel poori*[64] and we would be treated to this with a bottle of Fanta or Coke. We looked forward to our visits to Nairobi as we were also likely to get some chocolates from relations that we visited. At home we would get fresh juices, whatever fruit was in season, mango, passionfruit, orange, or sugarcane. Apples and grapes were a rarity which sometimes Kaka would bring back from Nairobi.

The big house had a sugar cane juicing machine. Whenever we had visitors, they would ask to be given sugarcane juice rather than tea. Also the other people in the town would send their servants to come and use the machine. I don't think they even needed to ask beforehand, they would just turn up and queue for their turn if others were using it. Similarly, Bapuji had also acquired an electric grinding machine for grinding wheat and millet and other grains. Again this was at the disposal of others in the town and I remember people coming to grind their flour. We didn't have a telephone but one of our neighbours, Kaka's cousin, Raishikaka did, so if my cousins or sisters rang from London, they would call there and someone would come to fetch us.

All this indicates what a friendly place Fort Hall was where your possessions were shared with others without any resentment.

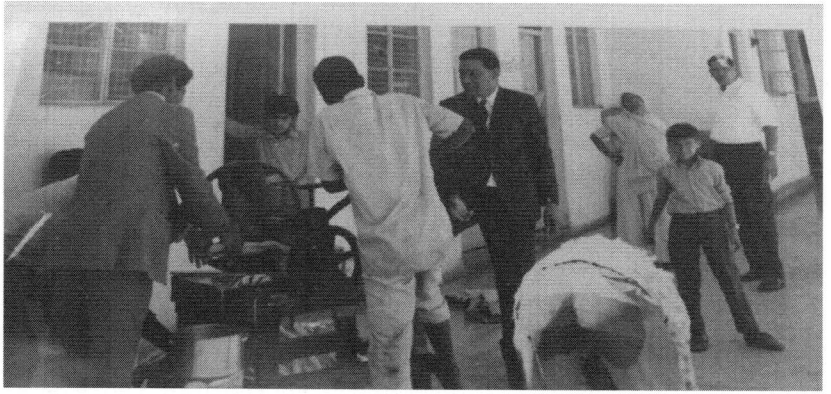

Sugar cane juice being extracted – Kaka, Shailesh and Motiba in background

---

[63] Uncle (mother's brother)
[64] Indian savoury snack

Kaka and Ba never hit any of us. I don't even remember Kaka ever shouting at us either. School however was a different matter. We used to get caned for the slightest misdemeanour and even I, who actually never got into trouble as such, was regularly caned, mostly for being late. It was an authoritarian regime, where you were not allowed to question anything but accept everything. The teachers were treated like demi-gods and were given absolute power which they sometimes abused. There was an incident where one of the teachers, made me take off my shirt in front of the whole class (it was a mixed school) and then scratched my back violently with her long nails for answering a question incorrectly. My back was very tender and it burned when I had a warm shower. But I was not the only one to be singled out. Lots of children got scratched or pinched by her; she was particularly masochistic and even used to read us gory stories of bloodthirsty savages that gave us awful nightmares. But still all of us wanted to go to school and I can't remember us ever playing truant. The desire to succeed and excel had been instilled in us at a very young age and we all worked diligently without our parents ever having to nag us about doing our homework.

When we were naughty, we were sometimes made to do *oothbes*[65]. Now renamed super brain yoga, this is getting a lot of attention from journalists and celebrities alike as it supposedly increases brain power and stops dementia. We have been doing this for years; if we had known of these benefits then, we would have been naughtier!

Diwali was by far my favourite festival. Kaka would get us fireworks and Shailesh and I would carefully divide these up between us. Most fireworks were atom bomb type that exploded and made a huge noise rather being spectacular to look at. For extra effect, we would light one of these and then put an old can on top so that when the firework exploded the can would shoot up and fly in the air. Sometimes we would even put this can with the lit firework inside on the road so that it exploded just as a car went past! I'm staggered that our parents allowed us to do this and it is amazing that no one was injured since again this activity was unsupervised. All the children would meet by the *derasar* and we would take it in turns to light our fireworks. All the men would be inside performing *chopda poojan*[66] In Fort Hall, only the men would perform this prayer ceremony, however here everyone partakes in it since *chopda poojan* is a day for everyone not only to reconcile one's financial books but also the spiritual books.

---

[65] Standing up and squatting down numerous times holding your right ear with the left hand and left ear with the right hand
[66] Religious ceremony during Diwali for closing of the financial accounts

The next day we would go and scour the streets for any unexploded fireworks and collect these so we could light these up. During Diwali and *bestu varash*[67], we would visit each other's houses and everyone would bring out treats such as sweets, chocolates or Indian sweets for us to eat. Ba would have made all the sweets and *nasto* at home so would be even busier during this festive time.

We also celebrated Jain festivals such as *Mahavir Jayanti* [68] and *Paryushan* [69] by going to the *derasar* and partaking in the *poojas*[70], and the *pratikramans*[71]. For Ba and Kaka *paryushan* was a very special time; Ba would usually fast on the first and last day but also completed *athais*[72] on a number of occasions. Whilst we did not always understand the religious significance of these, we enjoyed going to the *derasar* as it was a time of socialising with the community and getting together with our friends. We would get dressed up in all our finery. Niru had brought over a couple of dresses which I really enjoyed wearing during these times.

Close calls for Ba and Kaka in 1969

In 1969, Kaka came to visit England for the first time. By this time there were many families living in the UK and in our case all my cousins and Bena and Manjula. He came in the summer and visited a good few places in London including Kew Gardens where we have picture of him in a suit along with my cousins and their friends all in saris. He and Dilip also took the train to visit Gulab in Swansea.

Whilst he was here, he visited another of his cousins who advised that if Niru wanted to come back to the UK, provided she returned within 2 years of leaving, she would not need any other visas or need to wait. In Kenya, Niru had been advised otherwise and told she needed visas. Thus, she had already applied for the visa to come back to the UK. Niru received the voucher number and it appeared that she would have to wait for a while. There was only about a week to go before Niru's 2 years were up so Kaka telephoned urgently to advise Niru to come to the UK. However, just a couple of days earlier she had sent her passports to the authorities to apply for visas.

---

[67] New Year

[68] Birth of Lord Mahavir
[69] 8 day Jain festival of contemplation, reflection, fasting and forgiveness.
[70] Prayer ritual
[71] Prayer session to contemplate, reflect and repent
[72] 8 days of continuous fasting only drinking boiled water- no other liquids or solids

So Niru had to go to Nairobi and collect her passport. Here the authorities advised her against traveling without a visa and said she would be sent back home but she said she was prepared to take that chance. She had to buy a return ticket as no one would issue a one way ticket because of the situation and she came back to England with a couple of days to spare. She did not encounter any problems with the authorities upon her arrival in UK.

Soon after Niru left, Ba started getting stomach pains and vomiting. Kaka was still in England. Consulting the local doctor, she was told it was nothing and given some tablets. To ease the stomach pains, she used hot water bottles. After a few more days, the pain became worse, so the doctor gave her a letter to see a specialist in Nairobi. She was taken to Nairobi and when she was seen by the doctor there, he said it was an appendix which if not operated upon immediately, would burst and it would be fatal. This was the second time that something awful had happened to Ba when Kaka was not there and for a long time afterwards I would constantly worry whenever Kaka went away. But she was in time and had to have an emergency operation for the removal of the appendix, after which she recovered fully.

Kaka came back and then in September 1969, my cousin, Dinuben came to Kenya along with her 3 year old son Samir. He was so cute and cuddly and I would spend hours playing with him. He had this habit of throwing away everyone's shoes when they came to visit and it would take forever to retrieve the right pairs back for the guests.

The shop was still operating and Kaka would make weekly trips to Nairobi to get goods. Although Kaka could drive, we didn't have a car at that point and so he would take a taxi to Nairobi. The taxi would take other passengers as well so was not too expensive. We looked forward to his trips as there was always a treat for me and Shailesh, usually a chocolate, or some sweets, sometimes apples or grapes. On these days we would refuse to eat our supper until Kaka got home so we could all have dinner together. Ba would have eaten early as she would eat before sunset and normally we would also eat at that time. In Kenya it gets dark really quickly after sunset so by around 7pm it would be almost pitch black.

On this fateful day in September, we were waiting impatiently for Kaka to come and refusing to eat. Normally Kaka would be home by around 7pm so we were eagerly awaiting his arrival any minute as it had already gone past seven. The minutes ticked by and still no sign of Kaka. It was now nearing eight o'clock and we were both really hungry but we refused to eat as we expected him to come right through any minute.

Half past eight and still no sign of him. By this time we were getting a little anxious. Then around 9pm, a knock at the door. Someone from Thika had heard that Kaka had had a car accident and phoned Raishikaka in Fort Hall, who then alerted us. Kaka had been taken to hospital in Thika but had lost a lot of blood and therefore needed a blood transfusion. Bapuji immediately went with Raishikaka to the hospital so he could donate the blood.

Shailesh and I were stunned at the news and didn't feel like eating anything after that. Bapuji must have come back really late as we were too tired to stay up. They had taken Bapuji's blood but then decided to give Kaka just a water drip rather than blood. No reasons were given but I guess they thought he was strong enough to pull through.

The next day they released him. I had gone to school as usual and in fact had forgotten about the incident whilst at school. So I was chattering away with my friends whilst coming back for lunch and then as we entered our house, Ba said that Kaka was here. I was overjoyed and rushed to see him but I took one look at him and burst out crying. I was horrified. I wasn't prepared for the sight before my eyes. It didn't look like Kaka; his head completely bandaged up, from the neck up he looked like a mummy all wrapped up in white bandages lying in bed. As kids we always had a stronger affinity for Kaka than Ba. Ba would attend to our functional needs whilst Kaka would pander to our wants. Kaka would take us out, bring us treats and play with us, our feet on his feet he would hold our hand and swing us back and forth. I was not prepared for my hero, my role model to look like he did that day. I couldn't bear to look at him and ran out of the room crying.

Later I found out he had been sitting in the front and they had been hit by another car. His head had hit the windscreen and the impact of the crash left him with a gashing wound right across his head. There were 3 passengers at the back, another *Oshwal* with his son from Maragua and an African. The driver of the car, also an African, was killed instantly. The *Oshwal*s were not too badly hurt and Kaka still conscious after the crash, had asked the fellow *Oshwal* to take his goods as well to Maragua. The African at the back was badly injured and when a passing motorist was finally flagged down after over an hour, it was Kaka and the African who were taken immediately to Thika hospital. Kaka had lost a lot of blood during that time. At the hospital he had 22 stitches on his head and they had talked about a blood transfusion, but the blood Bapuji donated was not used on Kaka. The African who had been taken to hospital with him, unfortunately died overnight from his injuries. Kaka was kept overnight but then released the next day and brought home to recuperate.

For over a fortnight he had lots of trouble sleeping as a result of the injuries to his head but whenever he complained to the doctor, he was told it was because he was worried about his goods. Apparently the *Oshwal*s from Maragua had then got a lift from someone else and not taken Kaka's goods which were presumably then stolen. But rather than the goods, it was the medication that he had been given which was giving him problems sleeping. When he went to see a specialist in Nairobi, the doctor changed his medication after which he managed to sleep fine. So 1969 was another traumatic year for all of us but lucky for us both Ba and Kaka pulled through. To cap it all in January 1970, we received the notice advising us to cease trading. We had 3 months to wind down the business which would take us until March 1970.

The end of an era

So we began 1970 in the knowledge that were now in Kenya on borrowed time and as soon as we got our visas we would be leaving for England. Although we had British passports, these were British overseas passports and we all required visas in the form of vouchers before we could come to Britain, an attempt at trying to control the influx of immigrants.

The visas could take anything from 6 months to 2 years so it was a case of just waiting patiently for your turn. Kaka believed that if he had got his passport stamped whilst he visited the UK he would not have had to wait for visas. He had every intention of doing just that but he was advised by other relations that it was not necessary as he would not have to wait for visas. In the event, we ended up having to wait almost 2 years, during which time there was only the income from the letting of the shops.

On top of this, all the children who were studying in the UK, Manjula, Bena and Dilip were regularly sent £50 each per month. This money continued even though the shops were closed so it must have been a huge financial burden. But both Bapuji and Kaka were so convinced that education was of paramount importance that there was never any question of stopping, not even for the girls. It shows incredible foresight. In fact Manjula recalled that even when they were in Kenya, they were not allowed to do domestic chores as Bapuji would shout to Ba and Amritba and ask ' Haven't you got servants to do that. Let the girls study'. It shows the huge value he placed on education.

In the summer of 1970, Manjula, Bena and my cousin Dilip came for a holiday. I was on cloud nine, feeling really important hanging around with my older siblings. They indulged me and would take me with them when they went out. Not that there was much to do in Fort Hall, but I was happy just to be with them.

My older cousins, Ansuya and Gulab had also come to Kenya towards the end of the year to get married. Ansuya was already engaged (in fact Kaka was in the UK when Ansuya got engaged); Gulab got engaged in Kenya. Both of them got married within a week of each other in December 1970. All my other cousins and siblings were in the UK and could not come for the marriage so it was just Shailesh and me. Ansuya's wedding was in Fort Hall with the *jaan* arriving from Kitale and then for Gulab's wedding, we took the *jaan* to Nairobi.

Gulab's *mandvo*[73] in Fort Hall

1971 was going to be my final year in primary school after which I would have had to leave Fort Hall and go to Nairobi. I kept praying that we would get our visas before this happened so I wouldn't have to stay in a hostel in Nairobi.

---

[73] **Pre wedding ceremony**

We couldn't put our house on the market as we didn't know how long the visas would take. However everyone in the community that knew us was aware that we would be selling the house. One of these *Oshwal*s had an African customer called Benson Mogo who had several businesses and was on the lookout for a shop in Fort Hall. He must have mentioned to Benson that our house was going to be selling soon, at which point Benson came to Fort Hall to ask Bapuji if we were selling our house and for how much. Bapuji told him and Benson said that he did not need to see it but wanted to buy it and was able to pay cash for it, there and then. He said he didn't need the house to be empty and we were welcome to stay in the house rent free as long as we wanted but he needed the shop to be emptied by the end of the month. It was evening and Bapuji said that Benson should sleep on it and come back in the morning if he still wanted to buy the house at which point they would go and see a solicitor. So Benson Mogo bought our house without any haggling and we lived there rent free for almost a year! Kaka has a lot of respect for him and would visit him when he went to Kenya; Benson also visited and stayed with us in London and he also went to India and stayed with Amritba and Bapuji there.

In 1971 we made lots of trips to relations all over Kenya to stay with them and say goodbye to them before leaving for England. I loved these trips as it was the closest we had come to having a family holiday and I managed to see places like Marsabit, Nakuru, Nyeri, Kitale, Kisumu, and Mombasa. In those days you didn't need to go to game reserves to see the wildlife; you could just see elephants, giraffes, zebras, gazelles, roaming about in close vicinity of the road. We visited tea and coffee plantations, went on the beach, on boat trips and overall had a fantastic time.

The Kenyan schools run on a calendar basis and at the end of the year, I had to sit my CPE (Certificate of Primary Education) exams; By this time we had received our visas, so we didn't wait for the results to come out but immediately after the exams, we came to England on 5 December 1971 to begin a new chapter in our lives.

Fort Hall

Fort Hall school

Ba climbing up a derasar and ringing the bell

Ba and Kaka with Mama's family in Mumbai

Raishikaka, Bapuji, Kaka and others at Fort Hall *mahajanwadi*

Manjula made this cake for Shailesh's engagement

Kaka at Uttam stationers

Ba and Niru making *papad* in Mayfair Avenue

Kaka in a suit and tie at Raju's high school graduation

Kaka, Meena and Ba at Meena's high school graduation

Kaka feeding Ba after *athai*

Kaka with friends and cousins' sons

My cousins and their children at Zavbhai's house

England

To London (where the streets are paved with gold).

So on 5 December 1971, Kaka and Bapuji parted company. The 2 brothers had been together for 30 years but Bapuji, Amritba and Motiba were going to India after selling their house and winding everything up. At around 52, Bapuji had decided he did not want to come to England but wanted to retire in India.

Kaka was 44 years old; Ba was 41. Ba, Shailesh and I had never been on a plane before. I had even got a new passport for the journey. Motiba gave me a gold chain with a heart pendant. I was thrilled. This was my first gold chain and I wore it day and night. Shailesh and I were really excited, unaware of what was going through Ba and Kaka's mind. Especially Ba's. Here she was embarking on yet another journey where she did not speak the language and had never travelled to before. She was probably petrified.

We landed in England and at 11, I became the spokesperson for our family of 4, having already studied English, and being the most fluent in it. I was confident as I used to read so many books and considered my English to be good. However I was not prepared for the barrage of questions that came from the immigration officials and had difficulty in understanding everything that was said to me. Part of it was the accents and the speed at which everyone spoke and part of it was trying to then translate everything for my parents.

We finally arrived in our house in Forest Gate. My first impressions of England were not great. We had arrived in the middle of winter. It used to get so cold then in December, but the house in Forest Gate had no central heating; just some paraffin heaters which gave off an awful smell. Also the only toilet of the house was outside! This was certainly not the England I had read about in my books. But I was overjoyed at being reunited with my sisters again.

For the first time in my life, I celebrated Christmas. We had a huge artificial Christmas tree at home on the bottom of which my sisters and my cousins had put lots of Christmas presents. I received lots of presents and I just enjoyed the whole celebration. To top it all we had snow. It was a magical time, like the England portrayed in my books. For me the streets were paved with gold after all!

Quite what Kaka and Ba made of this, I have no idea. I was much too engrossed in my own experiences to understand everything else that was going around me. If I had asked them what they felt, they would be nonchalant, smile and say nothing; either they cannot remember or accepting their situation and suppressing their emotions had moved on.

In January I was going to start school at East Ham Grammar School for Girls where my sisters had also studied. A few days before I went to school, Niru prepared a lunch for me for which I had to use a knife and fork. I had never used a knife and fork in Kenya and was totally unaware of how to hold them. She taught me at home so I would not get embarrassed at school.

Before I was allowed admission at the school, I had to take a Maths and English test to assess my competency level and the teachers were surprised at how well I did. Even amongst teachers, there was ignorance as to what Kenya was like. Their books painted a picture of an uncivilised land where the lions and elephants roamed free and the natives were savages who lived in trees and drank blood. The gradual influx of Kenyan Asian immigrants had done little to dispel this myth and the teachers would always patronisingly pat me on the back whenever I got something right in English or did well at Maths.

East Ham Grammar was a friendly place and I fitted in without too much difficulty. It also helped that Bena was still at the school. However we were required to have school dinners and in those days vegetarian was a foreign word.

On the first day, I thought I would play it safe by taking a salad assuming that all salads were vegetarian. I picked up this innocuous looking plate with a leaf of lettuce, a few tomatoes, cucumbers and this thin slice of what I thought was a vegetable that I hadn't come across before. I took one bite of it and nearly choked as it tasted so disgusting. I asked the girls what this vegetable was. 'Oh that's corned beef' they replied, at which point I had to make a quick exit. After this I would stick to the boiled to death bland vegetables and the sweet puddings!

Before we had come to London, Kaka had asked my cousin to buy a house that was big enough for all of us. Zavbhai had originally bought the Mayfair Avenue property for his in-laws but when they did not want such a big or expensive house, he asked if Kaka was interested. The house was £9,000 and had been converted into 4 flats. It was ideal for our family but needed some work to convert it back to a house. It also had to be wallpapered, painted and have heating installed in it. Most of this work was done by Niru and Manjula along with their friends.

The house in Mayfair Avenue, Ilford was the house that Kaka and Ba lived in until their deaths. It was a large double fronted terrace house with 4 bedrooms upstairs and a through lounge, 2 reception rooms and kitchen downstairs. There was plenty of space for all of us as well as my cousins Sunita and Dilip and we all moved to Ilford around late January. I then had to commute by bus to my school in East Ham and it was a long journey entailing changing 2 buses, so we decided it would be better if I could get a school in Ilford.

My sisters did all the research and correspondence and eventually I was admitted to Ilford County High School for Girls, a grammar school about 15 minutes walk from our house. I started at this new school in the summer term so my 3 terms of the first year at secondary school had been spent in 3 different schools; the first in Kenya doing my certificate of primary education (CPE), the second at East Ham Grammar and the third at Ilford County High.

I was only given a couple of days' notice before the school started for the summer term so we did not have time to get a new school uniform. I went to Ilford County High for the first week wearing my East Ham Grammar uniform and was stared at by just about everyone- it didn't help being the only Indian in the class. Still, it can't have affected me too badly as I scored the highest marks in the end of year exams for both Maths and French.

Within a few months of us arriving, Kaka had managed to find work in a garments factory. By the time we came to England, both Niru and Manjula were working, but he still needed some income to support the rest of us. Unfortunately he was allergic to non-cotton fabrics and would come home with blood shot eyes. He managed to survive there for a few months before deciding to quit.

As he had some savings, he was not able to claim unemployment benefit or other income support. He needed to do something and decided that he would look to buy a shop; somewhere with accommodation upstairs and the shop downstairs. In the meantime, he attended evening classes to learn English. It was now my turn to help him with his homework; his spoken English was fine and I remember he used to go to Foyles in Tottenham Court Road to get the required textbooks. He would also get them for the other students in the class who were not so confident of traveling to the West End by themselves.

In early 1973, Kaka bought a shop in Plashet Road, Upton Park. It was previously an arts and crafts shop with cards and Kaka decided to turn it into a confectionary and tobacconist shop, with some greetings cards and magazines. The shop had 3 bedrooms upstairs so Bena and Shailesh went to live with Ba and Kaka along with my cousins Dilip and Sunita. Bena and Dilip were still at school in East Ham so it was easier to commute from Upton Park rather than Ilford; Sunita used to work near there. Shailesh managed to get a secondary school in Upton Park (probably one of the worst secondary schools) and moved to Upton Park. That left Manjula, Niru and me in Ilford. I was going to a very good school and it was decided not to uproot me again.

Niru was already engaged and about to be married. In 1972, she had gone to the US to visit my future brother in law. They had known each other in London and decided to get engaged. The following year she went back in June 1973 and got married to him. The wedding was a very simple civil ceremony with a few witnesses, none from Niru's side so the court clerk volunteered to be her witness. After this they had a small reception at home. None of us, not even Kaka and Ba were present. After the wedding she came back again as she had not quit her job. She used to work for the Bank of China and had been holding out for a trip to China for some time but unfortunately this did not happen and she quit in December and went to live permanently in the US. Once in the US, she used to work and then study in the evenings for an undergraduate degree. As a result, she improved her job prospects from secretary to becoming a certified public accountant.

Independent at 13

When Kaka, Ba, Bena and Shailesh moved out, the house was too big for the 3 of us, so we decided to have some tenants. We kept the large bedroom upstairs and let out the other 3 bedrooms upstairs to one family and the through lounge downstairs to another couple. The kitchen, toilet and bathroom had to be shared. Not a pleasant experience as it was always us who ended up cleaning the bathroom and kitchen. I got into the habit of cooking dinner for the 3 of us so that the kitchen was free for the other occupants later on in the evening. I learnt how to make *saak* and *rotli* at an early age!

I spent my teenage years away from my parents. I'm not sure that I missed them much. Manjula and Niru were there and I spent weekends with Ba and Kaka. Manjula and Bena had come to London at a similar age without Ba and Kaka, and at least I saw them at weekends.

I got on well with my sisters, respected them and sought their advice on any schooling issues. It was they who would come to my parents' evenings and other school functions.

Sometimes they could be embarrassing like the time when one of them was asked if she was my mother to which the other retorted, 'well I could hardly be her father'. When the headmistress found out that I was not living with my parents, she was a little concerned and called me into her office – 'so who looks after you then.' She was not impressed with my response that it was my sisters especially as I added afterwards that 'actually I kind of look after them!'

Ilford County High was one of 2 grammar schools in the borough. Academically it was a very good school and I was lucky to be only a 15 minute walk away, since some of the girls travelled from far to come to the school. At this school, I was allowed to come home for lunch or have school dinners. I chose to come home but was always rushing since we only had an hour for lunch. After a few months I got a second hand bike for £5 and then used to cycle back and forth. At 13, I learnt not only to cook but also to wash and iron my own clothes. We didn't have a washing machine, so we washed our clothes by hand, only resorting to the launderette occasionally.

Meanwhile the shop was doing fine. Manjula had quit her job to help Kaka set it up but it was not busy enough to warrant having 2 people full time running it. So she started another job and the shop was enough for Kaka to while away his time. When they got busy, usually at lunchtimes, Ba would come from upstairs and help out, more with keeping an eye as she still could not speak any English apart from a few words such as please, sorry or thank you. The only problem was that the shop was open seven days a week so they became tied up. We would try and help out at weekends, so that Kaka could go to the cash and carry stores to purchase goods. Normally one of us would also go with him; we would have to go by bus as Kaka hadn't passed his driving test in the UK yet and the rest of us were either too young or hadn't learnt how to drive. This was an outing in itself; there was always so much choice in sweets and chocolates and we would come back by bus with a few boxes each.

The company reps would also come to the shop and take orders and deliver goods but Kaka enjoyed visiting the cash and carry stores as they sometimes had offers and would be cheaper. Their social life was at a bit of a standstill what with no one living within walking distance, no cars and running a shop seven days a week. They were reliant on people visiting them and those that came would always be welcomed with open arms and rarely left without a meal.

Weddings galore

Niru was already married and by the end of 1973, had moved to the US. In 1975 Manjula met Mahesh and they started going out with each other. By 1976, they were ready to get married and so this was the first of our weddings. I had recently finished my GCSEs and was enjoying one of the hottest summers on record. Kaka went to India for a month to visit family and do the shopping for Manjula's wedding. I took on the responsibility of managing the shop. It was never that busy and I used to while away my time reading all the magazines, even reading the Gujarati ones. I really improved my Gujarati as a result.

On August 15 1976 Manjula got married to Mahesh. It was a traditional wedding ceremony; lots of guests, delicious Indian food, and a long ceremony conducted in Sanskrit that no one actually understood or paid any attention to. You just did what the *maharaj* [74] told you to do, whilst all the guests chatted amongst themselves. Organised chaos always seemed an apt way of describing these earlier Indian weddings. In those days, they were a much simpler affair. Manjula had Bharti a friend she had befriended at a bus stop, dressing her and doing her mehndi. Bharti later became related as a result of Dilip's marriage to Nilam, Bharti's sister. The *mandap* [75] again was decorated by some friends, and friends also took the photos.

It probably cost my parents less than £1,000. Nowadays, weddings are a big business as everything has to be done professionally to a high quality and the cost runs into tens or hundreds of thousands. The joke is you need to take out a second mortgage to get your children married!

---

[74] Priest who performs the wedding rituals
[75] The pavilion for the wedding ceremony, consisting of 4 pillars and a canopy

Manjula and Mahesh's wedding

My GCSE results exceeded my expectations and I decided to stay on at school for A levels studying Maths, French and German. My tutor had been quite keen for me to apply to sit the Oxbridge entrance exams but I was petrified that I was not clever enough and would not fit in. I had never even contemplated going to university until they started suggesting it.

So Manjula got married and moved out of the house. Bena had moved in to the Ilford house when she started going to college so now it was the 2 of us along with our various tenants.

Kaka and Ba still had the shop which was ticking along, not making great profits but they were able to pass their time there and make ends meet. They also had their regular customers who would come by every day. One of these was an old lady whose clothes had not been washed in such a long time that they were covered with holes from the dust and the dirt. It was difficult to say whether she washed regularly as her stench was so bad and you could almost smell the urine from her body. She would come in everyday and linger for ages to buy a sweet or so and take another age to give us the money. You half felt like giving her the goods and telling her to leave but Kaka said she was really really lonely and this was probably the only human contact she had. So my parents and us when we were there humoured and tolerated her. Then one day she stopped coming. We wondered how many if any went to her funeral.

Then there was another Gujarati family that started coming regularly to the shop when they moved in the area. The father had passed away, the 2 sons were working and the girl was at college. Every evening the brothers would come to the shop to say hello and may be buy some sweets or chocolates. Kaka found out that they were thinking of buying a house but were finding it difficult to raise the deposit required of £1,000. Dipak the oldest son, had tried all his relations but no one would help them out. When Kaka found out, he immediately lent them the money asking to be repaid when they could afford to do so. No official contracts, no strings attached. He trusted the boys and felt that he should help them out as he was in a position to do so. Today both the brothers are extremely successful and wealthy, but Dipak acknowledges that this was all started by Kaka giving them a helping hand. I only found out about this incident when years later I bumped into Dipak and he recognised me. He relayed the story to me and always had a very high regard for Kaka. Then in another twist of fate for a few months in 2006, he contracted at RBS on the same floor as me. He got so excited when I told him that Kaka regularly passed by to drop off some fruit and vegetables. The next time Kaka came, he came down with me and took Kaka for a juice to catch up.

In that same fashion, Kaka helped out others including various family members whenever he felt there was a need. At one time he was unable to single handedly raise the total amount that Gulab my cousin, needed for a business venture and so he phoned various relations to raise the required amount personally offering himself as guarantor. Kaka would also help out relations in India, including those who were very distant relations. Sometimes we felt that people took advantage of this kind and generous nature. But to Kaka it was always quite simple. He had a comfortable life and was able to afford to give. People only asked when they were in need and if he had the money, how could he refuse. It was hard to argue against this.

Since 1972, Bena had been going out with Vipul. She had first met him at an *Oshwal* disco and he was completely taken up with her. She was very confident, trendy and lively. On her first date with him she was wearing hot pants, high heeled boots and an afghan coat. How she managed to go out like that without my parents having a go at her baffles me. Maybe Kaka and Ba, new to the country, felt powerless to do or say anything. Certainly they were a lot more liberal than some parents today! In our early years they had inculcated principles and values into us and taught us right from wrong. Now in our teenage years they expected us to stay grounded and be sensible. Kaka especially was never one for lecturing, preferring to talk to us as adults and expecting us to do the right thing.

On 13 August 1978, Bena got married to Vipul again in a traditional Indian ceremony. Although they had been dating for a few years, she was suddenly overcome with nerves at the last minute. Nilam, Bharti's sister did the make-up and dressing for Bena. Bena was really ill with flu and kept crying on the eve of the wedding saying she didn't want to get married. But on the day she was fine and in fact hardly shed a tear at her *vidai*[76]. Again it was a traditional ceremony and there were a few white friends. Some of these had come all the way from Sweden; Manjula and Bena had met them some years earlier on their travels. They were trying to understand what was going on. I was assigned to explain the ceremony to them but I also had no clue as to what was happening! At least in this respect, we now have the ceremony explained beforehand and also usually the *maharaj* explains what he is doing throughout the ceremony and the significance of it all.

Vipul and Bena's wedding

---

[76] The parting ceremony for the bride who is leaving her family to go and live with her husband's family

So Bena was married as well and for the first time I was on my own in our bedroom in the Ilford house. I must have left the windows open and in the morning found a cat asleep in the bedroom. It was almost as if it had come there to keep me company!

I received my A level results and found I had been accepted at Reading my first choice university to read French and Economics. Suddenly I was terrified. What if I didn't make any friends? What if I couldn't cope with the work?

University and a world beyond my wildest expectations.

Too late to worry about all that. The first of us siblings to go to university, Kaka and Ba were excited for me but I don't recall them giving me any specific advice on what to do and what not to do. They were used to me not living with them and probably expected Manjula or Bena to give the parental advice. They were probably blissfully ignorant of the dangers and pitfalls awaiting novice students such as smoking, drugs and alcohol. Or if they were aware, they would have expected better from their children as they had inculcated their Jain values onto us.

So I went to Reading in September. I had one little suitcase to take which contained all my clothes and my books, some cutlery and crockery. A far cry from today! When we went to drop Nikhil and Arjun, the whole car was completely full! My cousin Dilip came to Reading frequently as they used to supply Indian dresses to a shop there, so he offered to take me. I was grateful for the lift and not have to take the train. Whilst there he introduced me to his suppliers who used to come from NW London to Reading every day in case I needed a lift from them at any time.

I was in catered accommodation and we used to get all meals six days per week. But in those days the food was awful for vegetarians, usually a cottage cheese salad sometimes for both lunch and dinner and if I was lucky some chips.

Apart from the meals I enjoyed university life. Kaka's income from the shop was meagre so I qualified for the maximum grant, yes we received a grant in those days! So I managed to live comfortably. Although I had been petrified before coming to Reading I quickly settled in. I made lots of friends as I was quite happy to make the first move, having always had to do that at school. The course was really interesting. I was speaking a lot more French and was even studying texts in French. No internet and computers so all our research was done at the library and sometimes we would be carrying a whole load of books back to our rooms; all our essays were handwritten. I had never studied Economics before but enjoyed the subject very much. I was loving the whole atmosphere of being at university and being a student. It was at this time that I met Hitesh who was working in the shop at Reading that Dilip, supplied dresses to.

It does embarrass me to say that I never expected or wanted my parents to be a part of the university life. They never came to Reading in the years that I was at university there and I never even thought of inviting them to my graduation. I would have been mortified if Nikhil or Arjun had done the same. Shailesh came to Reading for his degree and he did not invite them for his graduation either. This was left to the grandchildren. I asked Ba recently whether she minded but she was nonchalant. She said they had the shop anyway and they wouldn't have known what to do or say.

Meanwhile at home Vipul, Bena's husband had been losing a lot of weight and generally feeling fatigued. He was eventually diagnosed with TB and had to spend a few months in hospital. Bena had only been married a few months. Luckily, he recovered fully from this. Also around this time, Mahesh, Manjula's husband got burnt by a hot water bottle. He was off from work and recuperating at home for a few weeks but would go and help Kaka out in the shop. Mahesh had been working with the Inland Revenue but wanted to try his hand at business. Around this time Kaka's legs were getting tired from standing in the shop all day and so it was an ideal opportunity for Kaka to retire from the shop and for Mahesh to try out a new venture. He took on the shop on a rental basis from Kaka and Kaka, Ba and Shailesh moved back to Ilford in Mayfair Avenue.

A family holiday

The first summer after I started university in July 1979, we (Shailesh, me, Kaka and Ba) decided to go to USA to visit Niru. We were all so excited to go as none of us had ever been there. By this time Niru had a little boy, Raju, who was just over 2 years old. He was so excited to see all of us and immediately took to us. Both Niru and Manu were working and Raju was at a day care centre but when we went and dropped him there he would cling to us and plead for us not to go. During the day there was not a lot for us to do. Ba would prepare the evening meal and then we had a lot of free time. It was impossible to go out anywhere without a car and so the 4 of us would while away our time playing cards. In those days even Ba would join in and we generally played *chokadi* until Niru and Manu came back and brought Raju after which it would be fun playing with Raju.

At the weekends, Niru and Manu would take us to see different places and we went to see Niagara Falls which was breath-taking. It would have been even more spectacular from the Canadian side but unfortunately we were not allowed into Canada. Whilst our passports were British we had a right of entry rather than a right of abode. The Canadian government refused to grant us entry into Canada with those kind of passports. We had not known there was any difference and had never realised that we did not have the right to stay in the UK merely the right to re-enter the UK. I was furious as was Manu but it was pointless arguing with the officials. When we came back to the UK, I wrote to the passport office complaining about being treated like second class citizens and the passports were duly changed. It was this type of endemic institutionalised racism that was prevalent in the UK in those days. Were this to happen now there would be a furore in the media but in those days we tacitly accepted the situation.

On the way back from Niagara Falls, Niru and Manu took us to New Jersey to stay with some distant relations, Vijyaben and Keshubhai. They were really hospitable and took us to see New York where we visited all the famous sights such as the Statue of liberty and the empire state building. We stayed there for about a week as Niru and Manu came to pick us up the following weekend.

After a few days in Baltimore, Manu arranged a trip for us to go to Florida and visit Disney World. We, especially Shailesh and I, were getting bored at home all day during weekdays and had discussed travelling by a greyhound to the West coast. But Kaka and Ba were not keen for us to go on our own so Manu arranged the Florida trip. It was just the four of us. This was the first time any of us had been to a theme park and we loved the magic of Disneyworld. Even Ba joined in the rides. We loved going to see all the miniature dolls from all over the world in 'It's a small world'. At that time both Ba and Kaka were game for anything and we nearly all went to the space mountain ride. It was only when we read the small print that we suggested to them that they might want to sit this one out and let us go. At the time space mountain was probably the most terrifying ride around. It was pitch black and then as your eyes got used to the dark, you would see that you were going full speed hurtling down and the doors were closed, so you'd be screaming your head off and then suddenly the doors would open at the last minute! I'm so glad that Kaka and Ba didn't come. Shailesh and I were absolutely petrified and I just shut my eyes and kept saying my *Navkar mantra* till the ride stopped. We emerged completely shaken up with our hair standing and not able to walk or speak or do anything for a few minutes. We also went to Sea world and saw all the attractions there. For food we had taken some *theplas* and we discovered Pizza Hut; even Kaka had these pizzas. I think this must have been Kaka's first experience of pizzas, as at the time they were not very common in London and my parents never ate out.

We really enjoyed Florida and it was a great time to bond with my parents. Kaka especially was a lot more open to new things and I remember him swimming or at least paddling in the swimming pool in the hotel. Ba of course was much stricter with everything. She would never have considered wearing anything but a sari. With regards to food also she would not even eat bread or cereals so we were a bit concerned that she was not getting any hot meals; just fruit and *theplas*.

In those days at least she had more than one meal a day so that was a blessing. Niru and Manu also took us to see Washington Dc and Annapolis and so we had managed to see most of the East coast highlights. After 6 weeks it was time to say goodbye. Raju had become extremely attached to us and kept clinging to us and telling us not to go. It was heartbreaking to leave him.

In September of 1979, we had another wedding; my cousin Dilip's wedding to Nilam. Nilam had dressed Bena for her wedding day. They had a simple registry office wedding and Amritba and Bapuji, unable to attend the wedding, entrusted Kaka and Ba with fulfilling the parental duties.

Dilip and Nilam's wedding

Mahesh had been running the shop in Plashet Road for a few years and had introduced arts and crafts into the shop. He saw that there was a demand for this and wanted to expand into the stationery trade. In 1981, the opportunity came up to open a shop in Green Street.

This would be on the high street rather than in a corner and it was a much bigger shop. Kaka was offered a 3 way partnership with Manjula and Mahesh and he took on the challenge.

In 1981, Amritba, Bapuji and Motiba came over from India. My recollection of these events is vague as I was still at university. They stayed for almost 2 years most of these with Kaka and Ba but also with their own children. During that time my *nana* passed away in India. Ba proudly told us that *nana* had donated his body for medical research; after all the soul was gone. After this, she started carrying a donor card with her so that her organs could be used after her death.

Bapuji, Amritba, Motiba, me, Ba and Kaka at home in Ilford

Amritba and Bapuji had come to drop Motiba as she was getting elderly and it was difficult for Amritba to look after her however, Motiba had other ideas. Motiba was an extremely strong character and did not suffer fools. She had never seen eye to eye with Ba and was always criticising her. So she was not about to give in and settle in with Ba. She just staunchly refused and so when Amritba and Bapuji went back to India, they had to take her with them.

My year abroad

After my second year at university I had the prospect of a year abroad. I was both excited and petrified at the same time and I wasn't the only one. Other friends at university were even more scared than I was and one of my friends, Franca, who was studying French and Italian, told me that she was going where I decided to go so we could stay together. Part of me was glad but part of me wanted to be more independent so I could make new friends. In the end we decided on Montpellier simply because another girl in our halls had been there the previous year and said it was a beautiful place.

The university would not assist in finding any accommodation and it was left for the students to sort this out. Franca and I had decided to go a couple of weeks earlier to deal with this. Another friend Carole decided she would just join us for a holiday. No internet in those days so it was pretty much turn up there and see what you get. Quite what Ba and Kaka made of all this, I really don't know. They never seemed to indicate to me that they were worried, nor once discourage me from going. Even now when I talk to friends about my experiences, they are amazed at how liberal and open minded my parents must have been. Funny I never saw them that way. I always used to think they were very conservative but now reflecting upon all this, I really admire their courage for letting us pursue our education and giving us the freedom to do what we wanted to do.

That summer, I was talking to some friends in Ilford about my going abroad for a year and they told me that they had had a visitor, Jaya, who had come from the south of France. This was an unexpected surprise as I was also planning to go to the south of France and so I asked for her phone number so I could contact her. I thought maybe if I got lonely and craved some home cooked Indian food, I could always go and visit one weekend. I phoned Jaya and said I was planning to come to France to Montpellier for my year abroad. I could not believe my ears when she responded that she too lived in Montpellier.

She asked whether we had all our accommodation sorted out and when I responded no, she said she had a 3 bedroom apartment which she was renting and was planning to give up as her sister and husband had moved to Algeria. So she suggested that Franca and I could share with her. She said we need not decide immediately, we could always stay there for a few days and then if we didn't like it we could find something else. It was incredible! What are the chances of a chance conversation with a friend leading to a lady who had an apartment to rent in the same town we were planning to spend our year in? Some coincidences happen due to divine intervention and this was surely one of them.

Kaka and Ba were now relieved that I had somewhere to stay and although they had not met the lady, the fact that she was an Indian, better still an *Oshwal*, was a great relief. As it happened the apartment was 5 minutes from the city centre, spacious and the rent was very reasonable. So the first tricky bit of my year abroad was solved!

That year was an incredible year. We travelled a lot to visit all our friends in other parts of France and when Franca went to Italy, I went to visit her and travelled around Italy as well. We also met French friends who invited us to their homes too.

However, in the first week, I had a minor setback. Franca, Carole and I were walking home in the evening after being in a café. We were just nearing the apartment and I had noticed that someone seemed to be following us but was reassured by the fact that there was a car behind us as well. I was in the middle flanked by Franca and Carole on either side and as I reached out to get the keys out of my handbag, the man ran behind me, grabbed my handbag and got into the approaching car. I was devastated; my passport, my travellers' cheques, my credit cards and all my money was in that bag.

I had been in France for less than a week when this happened. God only knows what anguish Kaka and Ba went through when I informed them of my situation and asked them to send me some money.

Lucky for me that Jaya was there to help sort out things; we would have to go to Marseille for the passports. However when we went to the local police station they advised that generally in such situations the bag would turn up intact with everything else minus the money. And they were right! After a few days when we went to the lost and found property section of the police station there were literally hundreds of bags and mine was amongst them with the credit cards and passport still in there!

The year abroad went far too quickly. This was when I met Indira, one of Jaya's cousins and with whom we still keep in touch. Lots of people came to visit me including Hitesh for my 21st birthday, Bena and Vipul, and also Shailesh. When Hitesh came, we went to Andorra for the weekend on a university skiing trip. Hiring some skis and boots and clad in jeans and a jumper, we would walk up a few metres and then attempt to ski down. We only figured out later that we weren't supposed to walk up but take the chair lift up! It was fun even though it was hard work walking up and as we hadn't yet mastered the knack of stopping, we had to fall down when we wanted to stop!

I never thought about inviting Kaka and Ba and they never expressed any interest in coming to visit me. I recently asked Ba whether she ever felt excluded since she had never visited me at university or in France. She replied that Kaka was still working in the shop at the time and they were far too busy in their own things. They never considered it and I never thought about including them. This was still the time when I wasn't completely ready to accept my parents for who they were. This was the time that I was ready to forsake my culture and embrace the Western culture and Ba and Kaka didn't have a place in that part of my life. Unfortunately I will never know how Kaka felt about not being included. Maybe Kaka did mind. But if he did, he never gave us any hints about it. When both Nikhil and Arjun were at university, I would chastise them if I hadn't heard from them for 2 days. I still expect to play a major and active role in their lives and it is only now I can now truly appreciate what being excluded from a part of your child's life means. And I do mind.

Yes I mind very much. So my guess is that probably Kaka did mind. Probably he felt hurt. Again I feel ashamed for my selfish and inconsiderate youth. I wish I had talked to Kaka about this before he passed away. Now it is too late and I'm left with this guilt.

My wedding

University was a truly wonderful experience. I asked Bena, Vipul, and Hitesh to my graduation. I had started going out with Hitesh from my first year at Reading. Hitesh was working in a gift shop in Reading who Dilip used to supply dresses to. He introduced me to them, in case I ever needed a lift to London. So it was that I came back with them for the Xmas holidays and Hitesh and I got chatting and the rest as they say is history! Well, not quite. You see I knew that Hitesh was an *Oshwal* – marrying anyone outside the community was still taboo. What I didn't know was that he was related to me. So when I told Ba and Kaka, they were not comfortable with the situation. You have to go back 6 generations but to Ba and Kaka this was still too close. And on top of that we were related from the paternal side so had the same *attak*[77]. After I told my parents about the relationship and they were not too comfortable, we broke it off as both our parents were not too happy about it. But because I was still at university, somehow we started seeing each other again. After university, we carried on seeing each other. In the end Ba and Kaka accepted the relationship. Kaka never really went on about it; he'd discussed it with both of us and told us his views and afterwards respected our decision. Ba on the other hand was a lot more vocal and obstinate. She was probably also worried about what everyone else would think. At the time, I thought she was just being stubborn, but now I can understand her viewpoint a lot better.

What is even more remarkable about my parents is their attitude towards everything else that happened after we started going out. During the time that Hitesh and I were going out, his parents were breaking up. His dad was having an affair and there was talk of them separating.

At the time, divorce was a taboo word in Indian society especially in someone who had been married for so long, over 25 years and had grown up children, one of whom was already married. So when I found out this

---

[77] Surname

was happening, I was in shock. I just didn't expect *Oshwal* men to behave like that especially at that mature age.

I had a few sleepless nights before I talked to Bena who was equally shocked. She had a few sleepless nights too. In the end Hitesh and I decided to tell my parents before they found out from anyone else. But how to tell them. We told them that his dad was having a problem. They expected it to be gambling! No we said it was more serious than that. After a few minutes we managed to blurt it out and surprisingly, they did not seem as shocked as I'd expected them to be. Maybe this sort of thing did happen in our society and I'd just led a very sheltered life.

To their credit, they never used this against Hitesh. Never once, did they say that if the dad was like this, maybe the son would do something similar. Whilst they could have used this opportunity to make me break a relationship they were not comfortable with, they did not use this excuse to force my hand either way. For this I have the utmost respect for both my parents. They were tested severely and in my mind they passed this test with flying colours. When they were both resigned to the relationship, especially Ba, we decided to get married. For all the reasons above, it was always going to be a small affair. No big Indian wedding for me, just a simple registry office wedding and the reception was 200 guests. All the food was cooked at home by Hitesh's mum, and all of us helping. The invitations were from myself and Hitesh. His dad had moved out of the parental home by then and did not attend the wedding.

My wedding –Bhabhi, Hitesh, me, Ba and Kaka

Penances, compassion and charity in action

The next few years are a bit of a blur. I cannot remember what happened in Kaka and Ba's life and now they are not there to ask so the rest of the book is really my perspective and my memories.

Since an early age, Ba had always been extremely religious. A much stricter Jain than Kaka, she had never eaten any root vegetables, on top of that she would not eat fruits such as strawberries, and raspberries and vegetables such as aubergines and broccoli due to the amount of seeds. She would never eat after sunset. We could not understand why but she never ate bread or cereals. She cooked everything herself and a few years after coming to the UK had resorted to only eating one meal a day. According to the Jain calendar, certain days of the week, you should not be consuming any fresh fruit and vegetables.

She would consult her Jain calendar to find out what day it was and then decide what she could eat and make. If it was some auspicious day, she would fast. She would generally be fasting at least once a week, and by fasting she would not take any food, just boiled water. Usually if it was a one day fast, she would not even drink boiled water. Every day she would carry out religious rituals, *darshan*[78], and *samayik,*[79] and set aside a little money for charity. Twice a year, she would host the religious festival of *ayambil*[80] where she would invite anyone who wanted to partake in *ayambil* and she would cook the whole meal. She would cooks lots of different dishes, even though she only ate one dish, sometimes just plain boiled rice.

During the festival of *paryushan*, she would always fast on the first and last day, but on countless occasions would fast for the whole of the *paryushan* festival completing an *athai*. On one occasion, we were driving back from the hall after the last day of *paryushan*. Suddenly a cat jumped out into the road. Shailesh braked but could not avoid hitting the cat. The cat was still alive and Ba cradled it in her arms, wrapping it with her own shawl and willing it to survive by reciting the *navkar mantra*. We took it to the vet, but unfortunately, it died before we got there. Ba was distraught, and resolved to fast the next day in memory of this cat. Not only did she fast the next day, but after that year, she fasted every year on the day after *paryushan*. So she could no longer just do an *athai*; if she wanted to fast for the whole of *paryushan*, she would need to do a

---

[78] prayers
[79] 48 minute prayer and mediation
[80] 9 days of detoxifying the body where certain foods such as oil, spices (except for salt and pepper) and vegetables and fruits are not consumed

navai⁸¹. She also started to leave some milk out on a daily basis and a few of the neighbours' cats would come and drink this.

She made these penances look easy. Whether she was fasting or not, whether she was undertaking *ayambil*, she looked the same and would cook normal meals for the rest of the family. One time, immediately after Arjun was born, I went to stay with Ba and Kaka.

It was during *ayambil* and she had around 5or 6 ladies join her for the meals. She cooked everything for the *ayambil* and made separate meals for me; I was nursing Arjun so eating a lot. She also helped out with looking after Nikhil as well as with bathing and massaging Arjun. She never complained that she was tired, or weak. Fasting for even one day is so difficult for me; I am constantly thinking about food and looking forward to being able to eat again. I also feel lethargic and weak. She, on the other hand, seemed to get divine strength.

Initially when they were married, Kaka used to eat root vegetables so Ba would cook potatoes and carrots for Kaka and for us. Later, by the time they came to the UK, he had also stopped eating root vegetables, but she still cooked these for us. Kaka also started fasting on the first and last day of *Paryushan* so those days, the kitchen would get a rest. Kaka participated in the *pratikraman* during *paryushan* but not on other days.

Kaka regularly gave to charity; one of these good causes was a charity called BEHT which provides education and health relief to the poorest in Gujarat. One of his donations was to sponsor the marbles benches in the school in Chapparda. He donated the money to pay for a bench for each of us and our families, including one for Motiba. We recently saw these benches on our visit to Chapparda.

---

[81] 9 days of continuous fasting only drinking boiled water- no other liquids or solids

Marble bench bearing Kaka's name in Chapparda

Dahimasi and Swami Muktanandji, the visionary behind BEHT with Ba and Kaka

Shailesh's wedding

Amritba, Bapuji and Motiba all returned back in 1991, in time for Shailesh's wedding. This was the grandest wedding of them all. We had a week's long celebrations. All of us were present including Niru and family and we also had my cousin and wife from Mumbai come especially for the wedding. It was a time of coming together, of bonding and of celebration. There was much pomp and ceremony. We had singing every day at home for the week including *garbas*[82] and all of us including my cousins were invited for lunch and dinner every day at my parents' home. By this time, I already had Nikhil and Arjun; Nikhil was almost 2 years old and Arjun was around 6 months old. I hadn't yet gone back to work and so was able to join in all the day time activities.

---

[82] Gujarati folk dances

The wedding was held at *Oshwal* centre and it was a grand affair. Shailesh was the only son, the last one in our family so Kaka and Ba wanted to invite all the friends and relations. We must have had over 1,000 people at the wedding. Most of the memory of the wedding is a bit of a haze, however I do remember that we had forgotten to bring the pink cloth that is tied between the bride and the groom.

Indian weddings are such a ritual, so many different little things to remember. Ba had kept it safe but must have just forgotten to pick it up. It was only discovered when the groom was already seated at the *mandap*. There was panic and talk of someone going back home but that would have taken a long time. Niru, ever practical, decided that Meena, her daughter could sacrifice her scarf from her punjabi suit and hence for probably the first time in history, we had a green cloth rather than pink! It served the purpose and worked. None of us knew the significance of the colour; probably there is no need to have a particular colour. In any case the rest of the wedding went off without a hitch and no one was any the wiser.

And so on 1 September 1991, my brother, Shailesh, the baby of the family was also married. Kaka and Ba could rest now that we were all married and well settled. They had done their duty, the rest was up to us. After Shailesh's wedding, we also had the wedding receptions of my cousin, Zavbhai's 2 sons, Raju and Sanjay. Amritba and Bapuji had planned to stay for a couple of years so they were able to attend their 2 grandsons' weddings.

Playing *koda kodi*[83] at Shailesh's wedding

Shailesh and Alpa's wedding with the whole extended family

---

[83] A game played by the couple after the wedding to find a ring in a plate of milk

Amritba and Bapuji pass away

Amritba and Bapuji had come again with the intention of leaving Motiba here with Ba and Kaka. But even their meticulous planning could not have foreseen that they would not only leave Motiba here, but they were also destined to leave all of us forever. Amritba's death on 3 July 1992 was untimely. She had gone to my cousin Dinuben's house to help make some *nasto*. After dinner, she was feeling a little tired and so went to lie down on the sofa, saying she felt a little unwell, suggesting it might have been the *chaas* and telling my Rasikbanevi, Dinuben's husband not to drink the *chaas*. The next minute, she collapsed and whilst an ambulance was called straight away, it was too late. She had died instantly of a heart attack. She was 72 years old. All of us were in complete shock. She'd never suffered any heart attacks previously, she was not unwell, so there was no sign we could have had. Whilst no one had had a chance to say good bye to her, everyone acknowledged that she had been lucky in her death.

She had fended for herself till the end, even rolling out the chapattis for her last meal. According to the Indian tradition, she'd been fortunate in having a 'good death'. No suffering and no one had needed to look after her.

But she had left behind a dispirited husband. Bapuji was completely distraught at Amritba's death. Bapuji, who we had feared all our lives, who we held in awe and respect, was suddenly a broken man. They had been constant companions for so long, over 60 years. In that time they had come to depend on each other, had come to respect each other, dare I say it, even love each other. Yes I think love is an appropriate word. It is often said that in the West you marry the woman you love whereas in the East, you love the woman you marry. This is as true of Amritba and Bapuji's marriage, as it is of Kaka and Ba's. Theirs had been a completely traditional marriage, Amritba and Bapuji were both only 12 when they married. They both accepted their destiny and supported each other. Over the years, it grew to a kind of love, not one where they overtly showed any affection towards each other, but one where they cared for each other, one where they shared their chores and over the years got to know each other's likes and dislikes.

Bapuji, despite having 6 children, as well as his mother, brother and family, felt all alone. And so on 20 August 1992, just over six weeks after Amritba passed away, Bapuji also left us. According to the coroner, he too died of a heart attack, but I think it was a broken heart. He had been rushed to hospital but passed away a couple of days later whilst chatting to Kaka. So Motiba had no choice but to stay with Ba and Kaka.

Kaka holding Arjun, Amritba, Motiba and Bapuji relaxing in Dilip's garden

Celebrations and reflections

The following year, 1993 was Motiba's 100th birthday according to her passport. In reality Kaka reckoned she was a few years older. As this was such a special event, Kaka and Ba planned on a big celebration on 10 October 1993 by having a *jamvanu*[84] and inviting close to 1,500 people. This celebration was bigger than any wedding we had ever had and special cards were printed with Motiba's photo. All the food was prepared at home with the help of our family including cousins as well as friends. And then at the last minute, Motiba refused to come to this lunch celebration in her honour. She had become stubborn and difficult over the year; it was always easier for Amritba and Bapuji to get her to do something than it was for Ba and Kaka.

Finally she was somehow persuaded to come and in the event enjoyed all the attention she received. For the first time in her life, she received cards and presents. Celebrating birthdays and anniversaries was not done in the olden days. In any case you never knew exactly what date you

---

[84] Gathering for purposes of lunch or dinner

were born or married. We discovered these cards again recently. Kaka had still kept them all these years!

That same year on 24 April 1993, I was caught up in the Bishopsgate bombing by the IRA. This was during the IRA campaign in London to destroy the economic heart of the City; their primary objective was to destroy buildings and not people so they would phone and warn the police of a bomb. However a lot of the phone calls would be hoaxes designed to cause maximum disruption with minimum destruction. All the warnings had to be taken seriously as we never knew which ones would turn out to be hoaxes. I was based on the 36th Floor in the NatWest tower, now renamed Tower 42. It was a Saturday and due to work deadlines, I was having to work that day. Upon coming to work, I noticed road closures and remembered thinking there was going to another false alarm and another evacuation to the centre core. A little after I came to the office, the alarm went off, and so we duly congregated around the centre core, waiting for the all clear to be given. However a few minutes afterwards, the whole building shook and then we got told to stay put. We were in the central core of the building so could not see outside and this was before the days of mobile phones so we could not speak to anyone outside. It was a nerve wrecking few hours before they deemed it safe for us to walk down. Once we got downstairs, the destruction was clear to see. There were piles of rubble everywhere. The glass that was shattered was almost an inch thick. Downstairs we were able to contact home. Hitesh and his mum, Kaka and Ba as well as other family members had been worried sick watching all the news reports and not being able to contact me. We were finally allowed to go home after it was deemed there was little risk of cutting our heads from the falling glass. Nikhil, 3 and a half and ever curious asked me as I entered, 'mummy why did the bombers bomb NatWest?' Why indeed? We could ask the same questions today.

On 22 December 1995, the Green street shop, Uttam stationers was sold and Kaka could finally retire. A few years earlier, Mahesh had bought another shop in Upton Lane (Kaka was not a partner in this) and he still carried on running this for a few more years. However Kaka had been getting tired of late.

At the end of January, he decided to go to Kenya for a couple of weeks with Keshubhai, (his cousin's son, but more a friend); Ba did not want to go. They went for the opening of the new *Oshwal mahajanwadi*[85] in Nairobi and from Kaka's diaries of the time, had a brilliant time at the

---

[85] Community centre

mahajanwadi meeting lots of people and seeing the religious play 'Amarkumar.' Kaka also travelled to Mombasa for some sightseeing and meeting up with friends and family and he even visited Fort Hall, Maragua and Saba Saba.

Kaka in Mombasa with Keshubhai, Ansuya and others

1996 was going to be a golden wedding anniversary for Kaka and Ba. Initially, we, the children, decided on a surprise celebration for them but we realised it was going to be too difficult to plan and organise a surprise and so we told them what we were planning.

By this time, we had already decided the format which was a lunch followed by *bhajans*. We had booked the musicians for the *bhajans* as well as the caterers for the lunch. All the invites had been sent out and we were all looking forward to the event. Niru had prepared a special dedication booklet for my parents for this wonderful occasion. The children (all of Kaka's grandchildren, including our cousins' children) had been taught '*Maitri Bhavanu*'[86] and were due to lead off the *bhajan* session with this song – a favourite *bhajan* of my parents and it would please them no end to hear all the grandchildren singing this so fervently. With all the final preparations done a week before, all we needed was for everyone to turn up on the day. Niru and family were coming from the States for this special celebration.

---

[86] A religious song of friendship composed by an eminent Jain scholar, Gurudev Chitrabhanu

We had a week's skiing to look forward to before the big day, so we left on Saturday 9 March 1996, preparing to come back on 16 March. The celebration was on 17 March. In those days, I never used to phone anyone when we went away. So imagine my shock when I came back on 16 March and phoned home to be told that the celebration was cancelled and my mother was in hospital following an operation on both her legs to insert metal plates as she'd been walking around on broken legs!

My mind was reeling; only a week ago, I had left her apparently well. What had happened? It was like the whole world had turned upside down. To add mischief to misery, when I went to visit her in the hospital on Sunday, she appeared to have lost it. She remembered me and wanted me to give her some water, but when I went to offer her the water she threw the glass away from her saying it was poison and I was trying to poison her. Her arms were shackled and she had been put in a room by herself. Apparently the shackles were to prevent her from harming herself as she kept hitting herself. She had been removed from the general ward as she had been disturbing the other patients too much.

What had happened to my mother in a week? She seemed to have become mentally unstable. I tried to get her to recite the *navkar mantra*, the basic Jain prayer. But she forgot it half way and started crying saying she could not remember any more. She then kept pointing me outside and saying they were having a party in her honour but the nurses were not letting her go, and they had chained her to the bed!

Till then I had not realised how much she was looking forward to the golden anniversary celebration. She had never let on how much she had been looking forward to it. We had mainly organised it for Kaka as he loved these types of get togethers and he loved *bhajans*. Suddenly in that hospital room, it dawned on me that whilst she may not have expressed it, she had been equally or maybe even more chuffed by this event. Now, to her it seemed that the celebration was going ahead but without her. And all because these nurses were not letting her go!

That day I found out what had happened in the week that I was away; a short week that had sped past for us who had been away, but a long emotional week for those who were here. My mum had been complaining about her legs for a long time, but previous visits to the hospital had not revealed any problems. The day after we left she fell down in the bathroom and could not move. Shailesh took her to the hospital as she was complaining so much about her legs, however, again the X rays did not reveal anything. So after a few hours, she was being released again as they could not see anything. But due to some miracle just as they were about to leave, they were called back. A junior doctor had spotted something in the X rays. It turned out that her bones were broken in both legs and she had been walking around with those broken legs. No wonder she had been complaining so much. What amazes me is how no one had managed to spot this on any X rays before. Even this time, the experienced doctors had missed the signs!

She was then rushed into emergency and the following day, they operated on both her legs. For someone who could not speak any English, the experience must have been traumatic. She felt completely isolated and lonely. According to Ba, on the second day, when she was still sore from the operation, the nurse seated her on the chair for what should have been a few minutes but then forgot about her so Ba ended up sitting there for around 5 hours. The nurses denied this but Ba's pain threshold was always extremely high so the nurses were probably covering up a mistake on their part. After this she became a bit more vocal in trying to get their attention, and because of this, she was then put in a separate room and she was also shackled. Also she was refusing to take her medication. Ba who had not even taken painkillers such as paracetamol, was now being given ever higher doses of morphine to get her to rest and numb the pain. But her body was not used to all these drugs and she was fighting them.

She kept asking us why she could not come home. She just wanted to come home. But the hospital was never going to release her in her present condition. Someone from the mental hospital came to assess her state of mind. According to him, she was mentally stable but because of the drugs she was probably hallucinating. That was a relief. So we asked the doctors to reduce the dosage and by some miracle she became normal again after a few days. For a long time afterwards she kept muttering about the nurses being cruel towards her and someone from the TV channels had interviewed her with a view to making a documentary on this. For her this was real for a long time, but in the end this memory faded and we did not bring it up.

Unfortunately the golden wedding lunch and *bhajans* were cancelled. We did intend to keep them at a later date, but somehow this never happened. We were initially too wrapped up in her recovery and afterwards the timing never seemed to be right.

During Ba's operation, Motiba had gone to Zavbhai. Motiba had been wanting to come back home and after Ba came home and was well enough, Motiba came back. For breakfast, Motiba would want either *theplas* or *parathas*. Ba tried to get her to eat porridge but she said she didn't enjoy porridge.

So Ba would make a couple of *theplas* or *parathas* only for Motiba. Obviously this unhealthy fried oily diet suited her since she was reasonably well till the end. It was only the last few months that she was bed ridden but mentally Motiba was completely alert.

In the end she was taken to hospital for a few days, no one believing this was going to be the end, since we'd had so many false alarms before. Kaka told me that a couple of times he'd rushed to India on the news that she was on her death bed only to see her fully recover again and be fighting fit. However this time the end was nigh; she was 103 at least so she'd had a good innings and finally passed away in hospital on 22 October 1996. The funeral was not a sombre affair but a time to rejoice and celebrate. She'd seen grandchildren and great grandchildren get married and have children, so she was a great great grandmother. How many people can lay claim to that!

Holidays and more holidays

With Motiba now gone, and Ba recovering well, it was an opportune time for Ba and Kaka to go on holidays especially as Kaka had now officially retired from the business as well. Manjula and Mahesh were still carrying on but Kaka was nearly 70 and his legs were hurting from all the standing. He had terrible varicose veins which had been operated.

During his time in the shop, they had taken some holidays; Ba and Kaka had gone for a month's pilgrimage to India and seen all the Jain temples when Amritba, Bapuji and Motiba were still in India. They had travelled everywhere by train and had had a wonderful time.

Then in November 1993, after Motiba's 100 year celebration, Hitesh and Kaka had gone to India for 3 weeks. Both had eye problems - according to Moorfields, Kaka had cataracts, but due to glaucoma, one of his eyes was damaged and operating on the cataract would not fully restore the vision; Hitesh had suddenly woken up one morning in February 1989 unable to see out of his left eye.

It turned out he had a hole in the retina, the only explanation given was that he was probably having a very vivid dream and as a result it burned a hole. Moorfields had taken a few years to decide there was nothing more that could be done. So Kaka persuaded Hitesh to go to India and have both their eyes checked out.

They went to an eye specialist in Ahmedabad who took 400 rupees and confirmed within a day what Moorfields had taken a couple of years for

Hitesh. There was no hope in the damaged eye for him; for Kaka they said they could operate and he would get some vision back, but he would not be able to fly for at least a month. Kaka was not keen on recuperating in India for that length of time and decided he would have the surgery at Moorfields when he returned back to the UK.

With this taken care of, they had a couple of weeks to sight see and went to Palitana, Jamnagar, Mount Abu, Udaipur, Jaipur and Agra. Hitesh also went to Goa by himself as by this time, Kaka was a bit tired of all the traveling and rested in Mumbai. They had a wonderful time and to this day Hitesh cherishes his first trip to India with Kaka

In June 1995, Kaka went to the US for Raju's high school graduation. Raju was the valedictorian for the school, having secured a place at Yale and it was a proud moment for Kaka to see how well his grandchild was doing. Kaka also had the honour of accepting some of Raju's numerous awards. Unfortunately Ba could not go since Motiba was still around. Kaka was thrilled to be present, wearing a suit and tie for the occasion. He would normally wear a suit but he hardly ever wore a tie. He also attended the Jaina convention where he was impressed with the organisation of the event. A few years later, both Kaka and Ba attended Meena's high school graduation.

Over Easter a sports tournament takes place in Kenya on an annual basis for the *Oshwal* community, where all the teams of towns from Kenya meet and compete. It is a wonderful tournament that the whole community of the hosting town participates in; during the 4 days, all the meals are laid on, there is entertainment in the evenings and the games are generally played in a sporting manner.

It is a huge celebration like being in a carnival; the atmosphere is festive and friendly and the games are another excuse for a big party and get together.

Hitesh and I had gone to Mombasa in 1985, our first time of returning back to Kenya since we had come to England. It was all of these things and more. We had over 40 people in the UK team and were treated like royalty. The whole town of Mombasa had come to welcome us at the airport when we arrived and everyone there was happy to have us staying at their house. After the games, we went on a safari, our first, since we'd never done this whilst living in Kenya. We had also attempted to climb Mount Kenya on that trip and failed at the last hurdle due to terrible weather.

Memories of this trip were still fresh when the opportunity came up to take part in the *Oshwal* games for the 2nd time in Easter 1997. Lots of people were keen, especially as the venue was Mombasa again. We took a lot more participants along with their families this time, in total around 200 people. Hitesh and the rest of the committee had managed to secure a good package, so we had a hotel with half board. Kaka and Ba decided to come along as well since both Bena and I and our families were going.

Ba had not yet fully recovered from her operation on both legs the previous year. She had severe osteoporosis and was asked to take calcium tablets to strengthen her bones but the calcium did not seem to be working. She was having difficulty walking and there was a question mark as to how she would climb up the stairs. At home it was not a problem as they had their bedroom downstairs and did not really need to go upstairs. She was not keen to come as she didn't want to be a burden to anyone. But my cousin Ansuya and her husband in Mombasa insisted that she come and said they would be able to sort the sleeping arrangements and bring a bed downstairs if required. So they both came and it was absolutely wonderful. Ba, all of a sudden perked up. The sunshine in Mombasa was what she needed; all that vitamin D meant the calcium started working too. She had no difficulty climbing up the stairs and all the sweaters and socks that she normally covered herself in, were slowly peeled off.

We stayed in the hotel nearby but Ba and Kaka stayed with my cousin and then came to the *Oshwal* games to watch us play, where they could also socialise and generally have a good old natter. They enjoyed the whole atmosphere and it was humbling to see how easily they could be satisfied. They didn't need to go out to expensive restaurants or to nightclubs. All they needed was some company, for us to talk to them, play cards occasionally with them and take them sightseeing once in a while. Kenya was a wonderful holiday where Ba finally started her road to recovery after her operation.

Sachin's 2nd birthday celebration just before they went to the US

At the end of May 1997, Shailesh, Alpa and the kids, Sachin and Priya emigrated to the US. Kaka and Ba were not too thrilled about them going, but Shailesh had always wanted to live in the US and he had secured a job out in Atlanta. They lived there for just over a year but then came back in early June 1998. The lifestyle was good and they had settled well. Also in Atlanta, they had Hitesh's brother, Harshad's family.However they were still lonely there, missing the family here and the social interaction.

Sachin especially missed Kaka and would keep saying that he wanted to come back. Kaka and Ba were overjoyed when they returned back in June.

In June 1999, Ba and Kaka both went to the US for Raju's university graduation along with my cousin Dinuben and her husband. They all also attended the Jaina convention. They had an amazing time. Neither Shailesh nor I had invited them to our own graduations; we were just thoughtless not thinking they would be interested. And yet they went all the way to the US to attend Raju's graduation because they were asked. It makes me feel ashamed and sad that I did not try and include them more in my life.

Meena, Dinuben, Raju, Niru, Manu, Banevi, Kaka and Ba at Raju's Yale graduation

But over all these years, I was getting closer to my parents especially Kaka and wanted to involve them in our activities. Kaka loved it when we went to visit and could stay a bit longer so we could play a game of *bhukhar*.

He also loved travelling and kept saying that he wanted to visit Europe and other countries. They had already started going on coach trips to Europe with other people their age, taking their own food along especially as Ba was so particular about her food. But usually they cooked at these places and so it was never really a problem. Everywhere they went, France, Cyprus, Greece, Spain, they always came back saying what a wonderful holiday they had had.

In December 1999, we had the opportunity to travel to Tunisia. We had never been there, and I was getting a good deal on a package holiday. Kaka was keen to come along, ready as ever; Ba was not keen. We had our family, Bena and the kids and Hitesh's sister and the kids coming as well as Raju my nephew from the US. Kaka must have mentioned to Keshubhai who also expressed an interest to come. Keshubhai's wife, Radiatbhabhi wanted to come too and set about persuading Ba to come. Then Kavita and a friend also came so it was a group of 17 ranging from the age of 8 to 75!

And what a wonderful time we had. Except on the plane where Ba was sick throughout the entire plane journey of around 4 hours. She had had lunch at around 10 am that day as the flight was in the afternoon and somehow the food had just not agreed with her. She used to be terribly sick in car journeys in Kenya for a long time but then she had started taking lemon juice and effectively her motion sickness was cured. Until that flight to Tunisia! She was also sick on the transfer journey from the airport; nobody could believe she could take out so much. There was surely nothing more to take out. On arriving at the hotel, they were slow in allocating our rooms till Bena said that unless they gave us a room quickly, Ba was going to be sick in the lobby. So they allocated a room for her in double quick time. And she was sick again. Not a good start to the holiday as we were all worried and wondered whether it was a good idea to have practically forced her to come. The next day she was fasting as it was some religious day. When she fasted for just the one day, she would not even drink any water; on fasts exceeding a day she would drink water.

So she'd taken out everything and more and then she refused to break her fast to just sip a little water! Ba could be really really stubborn.

On top of that we decided to explore the beach the next day so we walked for about a couple of miles along the beach. And guess what! Yes she walked with us. If nothing else you have to admire her willpower for going close to 48 hours without any food or water!

We were lucky in Tunisia as we had some rooms with kitchen facilities. Although we had a half board package, Ba was never going to eat anything in the restaurant, but at least she could cook one decent meal for the 4 of them. The others including Kaka were however very accommodating. They were relying on me to tell them what they could and couldn't eat and were perfectly happy with some bread and fruit if nothing else was available.

Tunisia group except Raju, who took the photo

They were equally accommodating with the sightseeing; happy to go along with whatever we suggested, always ready on time. One day we went by train to El Djem which has a huge amphitheatre and they were happy to travel by taxi and train to get there. Another day however, we hired our own minibus with driver and guide and went to Carthage and Tunis. They really enjoyed this as we were all together.

In the evenings we used to sit and play cards, chat or sing *bhajans*. We never realised how much it meant to all of them until Radiatbhabhi passed away a few years later and the first thing Keshubhai mentioned to Bena and me at the *sadadi* was how she always used to say what a wonderful holiday that was and how nice it was for us to have taken them. We all thoroughly enjoyed the trip and for the children it was a time to bond with the parents and grandparents.

Writing about this holiday still makes me quite nostalgic. After the holiday, Kaka and Keshubhai kept asking us when we were going to again somewhere else. Somehow, nothing got organised. Tunisia was a one-off where we had a good deal and everyone could make it. After that we all pretty much did our own thing. It was a shame we never organised any further holidays like this with a larger extended family.

Kaka and Ba with Keshubhai and Radiatbhabhi on holiday

Kaka and Ba continued to go on holidays either on their own to India or with organised tours to Europe. On a lot of these occasions, Dinuben and her husband would also join them so they managed to visit a few countries, such as Greece, Portugal, Cyprus, and France. Kaka was ever ready to go, Ba a little more reluctant.

Kaka and Keshubhai also went travelling together when Ba no longer wanted to go and after Radiatbhabhi passed away. They took a coach trip to Italy and won over the hearts of the passengers by supplying them with lots of food and being such accommodating travellers.

And so the years rolled by. We were all busy with our own growing families especially as the boys were turning into such super sportsmen! We were tied up in taking them from tournament to tournament at weekends so we hardly had time to go and see Kaka and Ba. But they never complained. They would make the time to come and see us. They also had a hectic social life as they had so many relations close by. Manjula lived about a 7 minute walk away; Shailesh lived a 10 minute car ride away. Dilip, Dinuben and Zavbhai all lived within a 2 mile radius. The closest was my cousin Sunita who lived on the same road as Kaka and Ba. Somchandbhai, Kaka's cousin's son and his wife, Shantabhabhi also lived a couple of roads away. Kaka would make a point of visiting Sunita and her husband Shanti as well as Somchandbhai virtually every day, even when it was cold or raining. Ba would sometimes go along as well. Other times Somchandbhai would come round so sometimes they might meet more than once a day. Kaka did not like sitting idle at home, preferring to go out socialising.

And when they came to us they had all the other relations who lived in Harrow to visit, especially Keshubhai. They would bring us bags of fruit on the train and demanded nothing from us. Hitesh would occasionally offer to drop them home especially if it was getting late but they would never agree. They were quite used to the train. Never mind that they had to wait for trains and buses; their time was not precious. But now I realise how precious that time was. And I wish I had made more time for them. But I also feel satisfied that we did spend some time together, we did go on holidays together, we did play *bhukhar* and chat but you always wish you had done more.

In August 2002, it was going to be Kaka's 75th birthday; it was also Manjula's 50th birthday and Shailesh's 40th birthday in September. So we decided to do a surprise brunch for Kaka and celebrate Manjula's and Shailesh's birthdays as well.

We had organised for all of us and our cousins to bring the food and we were going to do the surprise at Mayfair Avenue. However we nearly didn't pull it off as Kaka had gone shopping and afterwards was planning to go to a funeral. When Dilip found out that that's what he intended to do, he managed to somehow persuade him to come home first and then we had his surprise. He was really chuffed especially as we had *bhajans* afterwards as well. This is the poem that I wrote for his 75th birthday

TO KAKA

Although we always call you Kaka
And your grandchildren call you *Dada*[87] and *Nana*
To tell you this makes our hearts glad
You're the best father we could have had

You never got angry when we rebelled
Although you silently suffered, you never yelled
Forgive us for our foolishness
Thank you for your love and kindness

You cherished and loved all your children
Even the neighbours' kids would to you run
Now you are a Grandad
The grandchildren come to you when dad gets mad

Memories of early times may now be a haze
Of those bygone Navagam days
When you worked sixteen hours for a penny
And food to eat you hardly had any

From that you've come a long way
And it makes us all proud to say
You may not have had a proper education
But you can hold your own in any discussion

You've helped many strangers and friends
They will always remember your helping hands
Your willingness to give free advice
And your passionate resolve to steer clear from lies

We are proud to have you as our father
Though we may not call you this we'll never swap you for another
You are strong kind and wise
And thinking of your life brings a tear to the eyes

---

[87] Another name for paternal grandfather

In the summer of 2004, my Veljimama and Amritmami as well as my cousin Chidrupbhai came to visit. This was the first visit from Ba's siblings (not counting Amritba whose whole family lived here) and she was really pleased to see them. She became even more engrossed in the kitchen than before as she was eager to please and cook a variety of dishes for them. They stayed for around a month during which time we also celebrated Bena's 50th birthday as a surprise. This was some challenge and the game nearly got given away several times but we pulled it off and it was a complete surprise to her that actually we were perfectly capable of organising an event without her being involved!

Another panic

It was 15 October 2004. Kaka had arranged to meet me after work at Liverpool Street station to hand me a couple of bags of fruit and vegetables. Sometimes he would do this rather than come to work. He had phoned in the morning to agree when and where to meet him. And then he phoned me in the afternoon to let me know that he wasn't going to be able to make it as Ba was not feeling well; they had called the ambulance and were going to the hospital. I knew that Manjula was at a wedding so I told them to go to the hospital and I would meet them there. Kaka insisted there was really no need but for some reason I insisted.

Normally I would not have insisted so much and luckily I had no meetings that afternoon otherwise I might have been persuaded by Kaka. I had a nagging feeling, a sixth sense that something was not quite right with Ba. So I met them at the hospital and saw them patiently waiting. They had been there about 45 minutes already but no one had seen them yet. Ba was complaining about pain in her left arm and looked very pale and in a lot of pain. I tried to find out how long they would have to wait. No answers from the receptionist. Finally another half an hour later and she was taken through. The doctor asked me details about her and was making notes when all of a sudden Ba started throwing up. And as in Tunisia, when she threw up she really threw up. I was trying to comfort her and try and clear the sink and at the same time trying to answer the questions for the completion of the form.

After what felt like an eternity, he did an ECG and then suddenly it was all action. He realised she was having a heart attack and so was rushed into emergency. Initially they would not let me in, but she could not communicate with them so I had a rare 'privilege' to witness everything as it unfolded. There were 5 medical staff there, they administered a large dose of warfarin to thin her blood and lower her blood pressure. They had hooked her up to a monitor to see how she was doing. They said she had a blood clot in her leg and they were trying to stop it from reaching the heart. She kept saying she was feeling really dizzy and everything was spinning round. I started to fervently say my *navkar mantra* and praying that she was going to pull through. I was not ready to let her go.

When we were in the waiting room, I had alerted Shailesh and Bena that I was in the hospital but at that stage we did not know the severity of the situation. In the middle of the emergency room, the phone suddenly rang. I had forgotten to switch it off. I quickly rushed outside and spoke to Shailesh who was calling to find out what was happening. I told him to come as soon as possible as it did not look good. I went back into the emergency room, and was told off numerous times for not switching the phone off. There were so many doctors there.They all seemed to be panicking. I still kept faith in my *navkar mantra*.

Finally they got her blood pressure under control and she was no longer considered at immediate risk. However they wanted to keep her under observation and so arranged for her to be admitted into the main ward.

By this time Shailesh had arrived and was anxiously waiting with Kaka outside. It took a few hours for all the paperwork to be sorted. At last she got admitted into the ward and was there for about a week. They wanted to do an angiogram to see how blocked the arteries were but Ba was having none of it. She already had a phobia of hospitals having had one terrible experience. She was not prepared to have any more operations or stay a minute longer than necessary. Unable to persuade her to get it checked out, there was nothing the hospital could do. So they had to release her.

By this time Niru had also arrived from the US. But Ba seemed fine and carried on as normal. For a couple of weeks. And then she had another attack. Niru and Manjula and Mahesh had gone to the cinema and when they came home, Kaka asked them to call the ambulance urgently as it looked as if Ba was having another heart attack. This time she was admitted straight away. And she was not allowed to leave. She had to have an angiogram. The angiogram revealed that she had sustained some heart damage and had a couple of blocked arteries but luckily not the main ones. They suggested angioplasty which would put stents in the arteries that were blocked to make them bigger.

She was scheduled to have an operation at the London Chest hospital in Bethnal Green. The ambulance was going to take her there from the hospital in Dagenham, but I decided that I wanted to go as well. When she undressed to put on her dressing gown, I realised how tiny and petite she was. She only weighed 45kg. Over the years she had lost a lot of weight and we'd never really noticed. She was very nervous and grateful that I was there. But these thoughts were never voiced. She rarely expressed her appreciation out loud, it was silent.

We were there for 7.30am as her operation was scheduled in the morning. After she came out of the operating theatre around mid-morning, she was given a day bed to rest in for a few hours before the doctor discharged her. We were told she would be able to leave around 2pm. And so we waited. And waited. And waited. The nurse who had come with Ba on the ambulance kept complaining to me but she wouldn't go to the hospital nurses to find out what was going on. So eventually I went and was told the doctor didn't need to see her and she was ok to go.

So we got on with the business of dressing her. The nurse accompanying her didn't see it as her job, she felt the hospital staff were responsible, they wouldn't assist, so eventually I decided to take matters in my own hands and helped her sit up. Then I got a shock! The whole sheet was covered in blood. She had been taped up from the operation, but she hadn't stopped bleeding. I nearly fainted. And I couldn't get either the hospital staff or the nurse accompanying her to take any action. So I lost my temper and started shouting, at which point the hospital staff arranged for a nurse to put more dressing and we waited a few more hours.

After this, she was ok and was finally discharged around 5.30pm. I let her go in the ambulance and said I would go home on the train. She was anxious about going on her own in the ambulance. She really wanted me to accompany her but I wasn't allowed. So we went our separate ways. The operation was successful but she had to stay in the hospital for a few more days till she recovered fully.

Funerals, weddings and other celebrations

Ba made a full recovery and was back to her usual self, complaining about the medication she needed to take and declaring in her stubborn way that there was nothing wrong with her. But it had shaken her. The operation had taken place around late November and following her return home, she had been told to exercise. So she stuck religiously to this task. She would walk round and round the house. She would complete may be 30-40 rounds.

Usually over the Christmas period we would have a get together so that the extended family could meet and socialise and play cards. We were at Ba and Kaka's house on Boxing Day and playing cards. Ba would never join us. She was quite content to be a loner and do her own thing. The kids had the TV on in the next room and she was doing her walking. Then she kept saying something about how all these people had died and she kept praying. It was only a little while later when we finished our game of *bhukhar*, that we watched the news and realised that a large tsunami had hit Indonesia, Sri Lanka, India, Thailand and so many people were dead and missing. It was absolutely awful to see all the devastation. All my 3 sisters' husbands along with some other friends had gone to Thailand for a holiday. Hitesh hadn't gone as we had been to Malaysia and Thailand only that summer. There was panic as Niru, Manjula and Bena could not get hold of their husbands who were totally oblivious to what was going on until sometime later as they were in a different part of the country.

The following year, 2005, Hitesh's mum, affectionately known to all as Bhabhi, passed away. She had been shocked to hear about Ba in 2004 as Ba had never manifested any symptoms of heart disease. My mother in law on the other hand, had been ill for a long time and was on a cocktail of drugs to keep her heart, blood, pressure, diabetes, and cholesterol under control. She had been living with us for about a year or so but in February had gone back to her own place that she jointly owned with Hitesh's brother. His brother's wife was expecting a baby in April so Bhabhi had gone back to help out. Bhabhi first collapsed at the beginning of April and became unconscious at home. We were away skiing. When we came home, we got a phone call that she was in hospital and in an induced coma. We were all really upset especially to see her in that state, but somehow we especially Hitesh, were not ready to give up on her just yet.

Whether through our prayers, or through her determination to see her latest grandchild, she made a full recovery and seemed perfectly fine. And then suddenly on 13 July, a few months later, she just slipped away without warning. This was a shock to all of us especially as she had recovered so well.

Kaka loved singing *bhajans* and he would always carry a couple of written down *bhajans* in his pocket in case the opportunity ever arose to sing these. He had a melodious voice and a lot of people appreciated his genuine heart felt response to a situation. So it was that on the day of

Bhabhi's funeral, he recited the *Shanti*[88] when the body was brought home before being taken to the crematorium.

We had also had another scare a few days earlier in July. On 7 July, the day after we heard that London had been successful in its bid to host the 2012 Olympics, there was a terrorist attack on London's tubes and bus, with 52 civilians dead as well as the 4 suicide bombers. A colleague's sister died in these attacks. It was another poignant reminder of how life can be snatched away so quickly. For me it brought back memories of the time that I had been working in the Nat West tower when that had been bombed.

2005 was also the *Oshwal* opening of the *derasar*. It had taken several years to construct and is a magnificent structure with beautiful landscaped gardens. It was a fantastic celebration taking place over several days with lots of activities, discourses, plays and other festivities. You could buy raffle tickets to sponsor the event and if you were lucky, your name could be drawn to carry out one of the opening ceremonies. Kaka had bought raffle tickets in all our names, including the spouses and grandchildren as well and he had also bought a ticket in Motiba's name, even though she had passed away. And so as luck would have it, Motiba's ticket gave us the chance to carry out the opening ceremony on a *kadas*[89] on the dome at the top of the temple. Niru flew over especially for these celebrations. Ba was ecstatic and insisted on climbing up the precarious ladder single handed without her stick. We were all worried but she was unwavering. She had faith.

She was dancing with joy that day insisting nothing would happen. Ba's raffle also won her the opportunity to carry out the opening ceremony on one of the villages, for the village of Navagam, our ancestral village. This was at *Oshwal* centre where the gardens surrounding the *derasar* have the 52 village names dotted around, each village having an *otlo*.

It was during these festivities that Ba listened to the eminent speaker and Jain philosopher, Gurudev Chitrabhanu who talked about the horrors of modern dairy farming. Raju, my nephew, had been vegan for a number of years, so she was aware of the concept and would even make many of our traditional sweet and savoury dishes without milk or yogurt, however she had never been persuaded to give it up. That is until now. Chitrabhanu is an eloquent speaker and it helped that he spoke in Gujarati. So her mind made up, she became vegan overnight. She would

---

[88] Peace prayer
[89] Golden pot

still make *chaas* for Kaka but from that point on she never took any dairy products. She did not give up on her favourites such as *jalebi*[90], she just made them vegan!

Ba at the opening of the *derasar* in the UK

Shailesh, Ba and Kaka at the top of the *derasar*

---

[90] Deep fried Indian sweet

September was another celebration with my cousin Ansuya's daughter Seiya's wedding. Here also, Kaka was given the platform to recite the *Shanti* in his soothing and melodious voice. In November Kaka and Ba went to India, for Naman's (my Veljimama's son Dilipbhai's son) wedding. This was a grand wedding in Jaipur and they thoroughly enjoyed the festivities as well as meeting all the other relations.

2006 was going to be another special year. Raju, Kaka's first grandson was getting married in the US. Since 2001, Raju had been living and working in Yorkshire, so was frequently driving down to London usually twice a month to visit friends and family. It was on one of his trips down, after he had come back from wedding shopping in India that he had an accident and was lying in a ditch, unconscious. A phone call from Anupa, his sister in law to be, woke him up. Confused and dazed, he somehow called Mahesh, and also the emergency services. The police and ambulance came a little earlier before Mahesh could get there. He had glass in his face and wood in his neck. Raju had escaped serious injury by millimetres! The wedding was only a few months away. It was a shock to all of us and another timely reminder of how fragile life is.

We had an initial *lagnotri*[91] ceremony in the UK in April which was attended by Monica and her family. The wedding took place in May in Detroit. The *lagnotri* ceremony went off really well. Raju's in laws as well as Monica and her sister Anupa had all come down for the ceremony and whilst this was the first time that we were all meeting, the atmosphere was very jovial and informal. It was such a shame that the wedding was to be in May when all the kids had their exams.

And so on to the wedding. There were a few of us from the UK. Ba and Kaka, myself, Bena, Shailesh ,Manjula and Mahesh, my cousin Dinuben and her husband, my cousin Ansuya and her daughter Seiya as well as Manjula's friend Rama and her husband. We decided to fly to Toronto a few days before the wedding, hire a car from the airport and sight see Toronto before driving down to Detriot for the wedding. Kaka in particular was really excited to be going. He was going to have a holiday, he was going to be representing Raju's side of the family at the wedding and he was going to be spending quality time and hopefully playing some *bhukhar* with family. Ba was not that thrilled about going, especially when she found out that the insurance for about 10 days was going to cost her around £500, a small fortune and almost twice the price of the airfare! She kept saying that she didn't need to go.

---

[91] Pre wedding ceremony where the wedding invitation from the bride's parents is sent to the groom's parents

At the airport, as usual, there was lots and lots of food being passed around. I'm not sure why, but everyone always thinks they'll be the only one bringing food and so brings enough to share with everyone else. Multiply that a few times and you could practically feed an army. Still, in Toronto we had been not been planning to cook even though we had booked into an apartment, so the *theplas* were going to be handy for the next few days.

For some reason, on the plane, Kaka and Ba had seats away from the rest of us. We went to see whether they wanted to swap with us but they were quite comfortable there having made friends with the lady in their aisle who was being asked to try this that and the other every few minutes! Food is a universal language and even Ba who had not been able to converse with her could at least offer her all the different foods she had made.

In Toronto we had booked 2 nine seater cars; Shailesh was to drive one and Bena the other. Manjula, Mahesh, Rama and Jagdish were doing their own thing. We had booked an apartment in Toronto so it would be easier for Ba if we did not get anywhere for her to eat, to rustle up something. Not that she needed much, and everyone had brought enough food to last the full trip anyway!

In the evening we had barely settled in the apartment and we had some visitors. Upi, a cousin of mine and his wife Elena who live in Toronto had just dropped his mum to the airport and thought they'd pop in. It was lovely to see them after so many years. We reminisced about our visits to Nairobi; we would nearly always go to their house especially as his father, my Zavumama had a *bhel poori* shop and we could indulge in that as well as get some coke or fanta. It was a treat that we looked forward to as we normally never got to drink fizzy drinks or soda as we used to call it. Plus we could eat these snacks rather than the staple *saak rotli*.

Upi and Elena insisted on us all going to their house for dinner. We said that it was fair enough for Ba and Kaka but not all of us but they insisted so we decided we'd go there in a couple of days. One day we went to the city centre and visited some shopping malls (it was raining most of the time) and then went to a lovely vegetarian restaurant. Another evening we went to Upi and Elena's for dinner. She had made so much food; separate meals for us and *saak* and *rotli* for Ba and Kaka. It was a lovely evening and they were both so welcoming. It had caused a certain amount of consternation when Upi had married outside the community but as I remarked to Kaka afterwards, she was a lot more welcoming and had made more of an effort than probably someone from within our community might have made. He totally agreed.

Detriot was about 5 hours' drive away but with the immigration controls, it took us nearer seven. They detained us for a little longer as Shailesh had not surrendered his green card yet; they had all that on file. They could not understand why anyone would choose not to live in the US, so questioned him for over an hour. They realised from our passports that we were born in Kenya and from our colour that we were Indian, so assumed that Kenya must be in India! Hopefully they are now better informed!

During the long drive, we would communicate between the 2 cars via walkie talkies and at one point started singing wedding songs for the other car to hear. We reached the hotel just before evening. The hotel was really plush with 2 double beds in each room and fruit baskets as a welcome gift. The guests began arriving in the evening ahead of the whole programme starting the next day on Saturday. On Friday evening there was a dinner for just the groom's side after which we sang a few wedding songs. Niru was really organised and had printed off lots of booklets of all our favourite well known wedding songs personalised for all the names to be sung.

Saturday morning was the *pooja* at the Jain *derasar* followed by lunch. It was a beautiful *pooja* with everyone listening attentively and the lunch was delicious. All the food had been made to the lowest common denominator, Jain vegan. In the evening we had a *sangeet sandhya*[92] which was really fabulous, very glitzy, ably compered by Meena (my niece, Raju's sister) and Anupa (Monica's sister). Kaka had been asked to give a speech as had I. Kaka had been in a bit of a quandary as to what to write and I had written something for him which was quite funny about never arguing with women and that he had had enough experience of this what with a wife and 4 daughters. Dinuben however felt it was not appropriate and cancelled that bit out. It was a shame as there were lots of funny jokes and it would have been quite suitable. So instead he spoke about equanimity and about joy and sorrow and keeping both of these in check, never getting too elated in times of happiness and never losing hope in times of sorrow.

He was really nervous delivering it. This was the first time I had seen him so nervous, maybe because it was a totally new audience. The speeches were followed by music and dancing until the early hours.

---

[92] Pre wedding fun event comprising of music, dancing and speeches

The food at the evening was extravagant; so many different stations serving Mumbai street food, south Indian, Chinese, Mexican. And the desserts were so tempting! Again everything Jain vegan

The next day was the wedding. We had a *dhol*[93] playing and we all danced our way to the wedding ceremony in true *jaan* style. It had threatened to rain but we were lucky. The wedding itself was a beautiful ceremony conducted in pin drop silence. The *maharaj* explained everything in English so we could all understand what was going on. Some more speeches after the wedding and then another lavish meal with so much variety. We were all really impressed not so much with the lavish wedding but more with the warm welcome we had received from Monica's family. They had truly made the ordinary, extraordinary! Ba and Kaka too were humbled by the experience but they never showed too much emotion. Somehow they always kept their emotions in check. It was like in Kaka's speech; don't get too elated when you're happy, don't get too dejected when you're sad. Life will always give you these ups and downs. The important thing is to stay detached.

We on the other hand were totally elated and I kept thinking that we should somehow reciprocate but was at a loss as to what. It had also been Monica's parents wedding anniversary that Sunday making the day even more special. The next day we had been invited to brunch at Monica's parents' home before we headed off to Toronto again. I had been racking my brains the night before and came up with a thank you poem that I thought would be appropriate to share at this brunch. The brunch again was very special and sharing this thank you poem with Monica's family was well received.

---

[93] Indian drum

Raju and Monica's wedding

After a wonderful breakfast, it was back on the road again to Toronto. We visited Niagara Falls; although we've been a few times, it is still awe inspiring to witness the sheer power of nature, watching the water gushing so fast and hearing the thunderous roar of these majestic waterfalls.

We also visited an Indian vegetarian restaurant; probably the first time for Ba, where we all had a lovely meal. On our last day we all went to visit one of the islands off Toronto; it was beautiful, lots of walking and cycling opportunities. Alas we were nearing the end of this mini holiday. The wedding had been really wonderful and spending time with Kaka, Ba, Dinuben and Rasikbanevi and others was really nice. They all really appreciated the opportunity of travelling and being with us and it had turned out to be a great bonding session for all.

So it was back to the UK, back to work and back to the routine. Nikhil was sitting his GCSE's and Arjun had his internal exams. But there was a wedding reception planned in the UK in June so we had the opportunity to be hosts to Monica's family once more. Only a few of us had been able to go to the wedding in the US. This time everyone could attend and although it was just the one evening, we had dinner followed by dancing to *garba* music which everyone thoroughly enjoyed.

During this time we also had a small family celebration at home for Kaka and Ba's 60th wedding anniversary. Somehow we had never got around to organising another celebration for their golden wedding anniversary after the original one had to be cancelled due to Ba's operations on her legs. This time we had just the extended family at home and below is a translation of what I read out in Gujarati. They both looked so pleased and were so grateful. It really took very little to make them happy; just the whole family getting together was enough!

To Kaka and Ba for your 60th wedding anniversary from all your family

Don't forget your Mum and Dad. This is the advice that Ba and Kaka regularly give us. But how can we forget such devoted parents.

Today we're all here to celebrate their 60th Wedding anniversary. Well only 10 years late, as previously we had made all the preparations for the celebration of their 50th wedding anniversary when with a week to go Ba was admitted to hospital.

But whenever we face any difficulties, Ba and Kaka always console us that whatever happens, happens for the best. So when we look at this celebration, we realise how fortunate we are that today, even Anjali, Monica and Monica's family are present here to grace the occasion.

Kaka and Ba you've always given us good advice and raised us with high morals. You trusted us and gave us independence and freedom to fulfil all our aspirations. You did not study further, but you encouraged us to pursue our academic education to whatever level we wanted to.

From observing your life, we are learning how to live a contented life. From seeing how you greet and welcome everyone, we are learning how to greet with open arms all those we meet, even though some may insult us or may not talk to us. As you often tell us we must never poison our tongues by reacting back. God likes us to be humble and take the first step towards reconciliation. As they say pride comes before a fall.

You have taught us never to cheat anyone. What is wrong will come to light one day, if not today then tomorrow.

Throughout your life, you have demonstrated to us the priceless teachings of the Jain religion. You have taught us that it is our duty to help those in need. Your greatest joy is in giving. That is why you always bring us fresh fruit and vegetables and make us delicious food.

So how can we forget these values and these exemplary lives? We may forget everything else but we will never forget you.

We pray that you are able to live the rest of your lives as peacefully and serenely as you have done the last few years.

Yet more holidays, celebrations and weddings and drama

Meanwhile my eyes had been getting worse. I had had them checked out at Moorfields but they suggested it was just floaters. I was finding it difficult to read; everything was quite opaque in one eye. Even at Raju's wedding, I had difficulty reading my speech. Manjula had been wanting to go to a health farm in India for ages and Bena, Manjula and I we decided to go in December. I managed to get some unpaid leave from work and we decided to go for 5 weeks; 3 weeks in the health farm and rest of the time in Mumbai. For a second time that year (2006), Hitesh was looking after the kids!

After a few days in Mumbai we went to Uruli Kanchan, one of the first nature cure places in India, opened by Gandhiji himself and based on his principles. Whilst fairly basic and really really cheap, it was clean. We were initially given rooms with Indian toilets but after some objections, they upgraded us. The rooms were ensuite but quite sparse and bare. The regime was fairly regimental; getting up at 5am and going for yoga, walks, massages, and treatments.

The evenings were spent chanting *bhajans* and then off to bed around 9pm. They could not help with the eyes, but I felt a lot better. Massages everyday released the tensions in my neck and shoulders built up over the years spent slouching on the computer and yoga and mud packs in the sun rejuvenated my body and skin. The bland food made us lose a little weight and all the other treatments toned us up and revitalised us. It was a wonderful experience; no mobiles or internet, unless you went outside, inside it was me time leading to a lot of introspection. We made a lot of friends, including a couple from Mumbai, an optician, who suggested an eye hospital in Mumbai for the eyes. The 3 weeks went by really quickly and all of a sudden it was time to return to Mumbai. In Mumbai we had already made an appointment with an eye hospital and I managed to see the optician, a cataract specialist and the top surgeon at the hospital on the same day at a total cost of around £5, who all confirmed that I had a cataract. They could operate in India but I decided to wait and have it checked out with Moorfields when I got back.

We also had a wedding in Mumbai; my cousin Shardaben's son, Sayam was getting married. Ba and Kaka were also scheduled to come to the wedding; just a day before the wedding, however they got bumped off and arrived a day later so on the day of the wedding and were brought straight to the wedding from the airport. They looked completely fresh and even had all the wedding food. The rest of us just tasted a few things as we had reservations of eating the *mahajanwadi* food. As Ba used to say *'kari kuti ne khai lo to kai ni thai'* (eat heartily and you won't fall ill).

Seiya, my cousin's daughter was living in Mumbai at this time, her husband having been posted out here and they had a plush apartment near the Taj hotel. Manjula and I had already spent a few days there and when Kaka and Ba came to India, Seiya insisted that they visit. So I took them there along with my Veljimama and they had a wonderful time. Kaka had brought his camera along and we have photos of Kaka, Ba and Veljimama relaxing by the pool and drinking bottles of water. We also went to a nearby park called *nana* and *nani* park.

Dahimasi's grandson, Sayam's wedding

Kaka had a love for travelling and had been wanting to go to Australia for some time, however it had never worked out. This time in India, my cousin Pradipbhai offered to go with him and so the 2 of them went to Sydney to visit Sanjay, my cousin Zavbhai's son in January 2007. Ba did not enjoy travelling as much and was quite content to stay on in Mumbai. Kaka had originally wanted to go to Perth and other places but they were only there for 10 days and Sanjay convinced them to stay in Sydney and took them to all the famous sights. Kaka had a wonderful time and proudly showed us his photos. Reyen, Sanjay's son became particularly attached to Kaka and used to call him *Dadakaka*. 9 years later and only Bena from us siblings has managed to visit Australia, and that only last year! When I reflect on this fact, I feel very proud that my father did so much travelling in his later years when he had both the time and the money.

Kaka and Pradipbhai in Sydney with Reyen and Jaini

Ba on the other hand, spent time in Mumbai with her brother's family as well as her sister Dahiben who had come from Jamnagar. My Veljimama, Ba's brother was very religious and strict and was also well read. He would often counsel everyone against the ills of taking medication; he used to say that it was white substances that you had to avoid, such as sugar, salt and of course all these pills that were generally white. It was during this time that Ba became persuaded to stop all her medication including her blood pressure tablets, cholesterol tablets and any blood thinning medication, much to our consternation. But steadfast determination was my mother's middle name. Once her mind was made up, she could not be persuaded to change it.

And so she gave up all medication and continued after they returned back to the UK. We would tell her off especially as blood pressure was deemed a silent killer and she may not get any symptoms.

She would respond she had no fear of dying. She had always been strong and was not going to be dissuaded by us. However, we did persuade her to get her blood pressure checked regularly which she agreed to. When this was repeatedly high for a period, after some arguments, she agreed to give up salt rather than agree to take any medication. So for over a year, she cooked without salt (adding salt to Kaka's food afterwards) with the result that her blood pressure normalised and she felt better without any of the medications! Something to bear in mind!

I had arranged to have some time off from work in 2007 from June to September. I had also had another check up at Moorfields regarding my eye. They confirmed that it was a cataract and the operation was scheduled in October. It was great having the time off in the summer. The boys had their exams. Nikhil had his AS and Arjun his GCSEs and it was wonderful to be able to have food ready on the table when they returned from school.

Kaka had been wanting to visit Turkey for some time and now that I had a few months off from work, Hitesh and I decided it would be nice to take Kaka to Turkey. It was just the 3 of us; Ba was not interested in coming. We flew to Marmaris and had a self-catering apartment for a week. Kaka was so excited about everything, especially all the fresh fruits! We went to this farm where they had huge peaches growing and we picked so many fresh peaches from there. We took a boat trip that included lunch; for us this was some rice and vegetables. Kaka couldn't eat anything as there were potatoes but was quite happily eating his *theplas*.

We wanted to take Kaka to Pamukale and Ephesus; we had visited these on an earlier trip years before and were really impressed by these sights. Kaka was quite happy with this until he found out that we had only hired a car. He thought the driver came with the car and was quite mortified when he found out Hitesh would be driving! The road was quite mountainous and some hairpin bends but Hitesh did well.

On the first day we went to Pamukale, literally 'cotton castle'. It is a wonderful sight of natural hot springs and terraces of white 'cotton' created by the limescale. To go to the natural bathing pools, you have to hike up barefoot; you are not allowed to wear any footwear to avoid causing damage. The path however is not easy as you are walking on stones barefoot and there is water flowing down the slope so the stones can be quite slippery. Kaka was getting tired half way through and wanted to give up but we gently kept coaxing him and urging him to go further till we came to a wonderful bathing pool, where even Kaka had a nice long shower! The waters of this natural wonder are therapeutic and we all felt energised by the experience. However I did feel guilty afterwards when back at the apartment, he showed me his feet which were full of blisters.

The next day we went to Ephesus which was one of the largest cities in the Roman Empire in the 2nd century. Now in ruins, it is still very impressive, however Kaka was not too impressed. To him, it was just a pile of ruins, he kept saying there were better ruins in India to see. Like a child bored after five minutes of play, he kept asking if we had finished! He just could not understand our fascination of this place!

The remaining days were spent on the beach or by the swimming pool, relaxing. It was on this holiday, that I began this project in earnest. I started talking to Kaka about his childhood; his life in India and how he came to be in Kenya. We were trying to record him on video but he was quite camera shy and clammed up. It was much easier to just talk and take notes.

All in all we had a wonderful holiday. It was a great bonding session and it was a pleasure for me and Hitesh to take Kaka with us and visit a country that he had wanted to go to. Once back, he was proudly showing the photos and video that Hitesh had put together to the rest of the family.

Kaka at Pamukale

It was Kaka's 80th birthday in 2007 and he wanted to celebrate it in true Kaka style, so he decided to sponsor the East area *savantsari bhojan*.[94] All the guests he had invited had come so he was really chuffed with the whole event.

Due to the cataracts, my vision was getting bad. I could no longer wear contact lenses so had to wear glasses the whole time. My 4 months break was up and I had to start work again in September. But finally my appointment for the cataract came in early October so after a few weeks I was off work again. They tell you not to do any cooking or go near the cooker for the first few days, so Kaka and Ba came to the rescue. They decided to come over and look after me for a week!

They arrived by train, Kaka carrying his usual few bags of fruits and vegetables, just as we were coming back from the hospital. Immediately Ba started cooking – *saak rotli, rotlo, daal bhat*. Even now when I think about it, I have tears in my eyes. It was a labour of love. They stayed for a week and it was wonderful having them around. My 2nd operation for the right eye was scheduled for January but then there was a cancellation

---

[94] Community lunch after the end of Paryushan

in November so I had it then. This time both Kaka and Ba were in India as was Bena. My *bhabhi* Panna came to the rescue and sent tiffins on a daily basis.

Whilst Kaka loved travelling and visiting new places, Ba was quite content to be at home. But visiting India was different. For both of them it was a home away from home. For Ba it was a chance to meet her family; her brother in Mumbai and her sister in Jamnagar. This trip in 2007/2008 would be the last time that they would meet as Ba never went back to India.

Chandubhai, Savitabhabhi, Dahimasi with Ba and Kaka.

In India with Mama , Mami, Chidrupbhai, Pradipbhai, Kusumbhabhi and Sahaj

Kaka and Ba came back in January and then in February Kaka decided to go to San Francisco to visit Meena, Niru's daughter. Niru and Manu were going to visit her and so Kaka decided to visit too. The flight was really long; he had a stopover in New York but Kaka was fine. He never complained about the journeys he had to endure, he looked forward to the destinations. Again he had a wonderful time there.

Meanwhile also in February 2008, Vijay, Manjula's son was off on an arctic adventure. He and another adventurer were attempting to cross the penny ice cap on Baffin Island. They would be sleeping in tents in temperatures of -35C. Vijay was into trekking and had been on lots of mountaineering expeditions and other trekking adventures, however this was a whole new level. Kaka and Ba, who used to think skiing, was dangerous and 'about breaking a leg', thought he was mad to undertake such a crazy adventure. They felt he should be dissuaded. They thought it was foolhardy and were worried Vijay would not survive in such a harsh, hostile and isolated environment. However, Vijay was determined and Manjula and Mahesh supported Vijay; it was a chance to make history.

Unfortunately a few days into the crossing attempt, Vijay and Anthony were forced to turn back due to Vijay getting frostbite. They were sensible in turning back at the right time; he could have lost his toes if he had stayed longer in such cold temperatures. Kaka was vindicated and felt justified for being opposed to Vijay going.

But in 2011, on his second attempt, Vijay did succeed. Kaka would have been proud to learn that Vijay was part of a 3 man team, the first British team, to traverse the penny ice cap on Baffin Island. It was a really tough challenge in harsh conditions but he had made history!

In 2008 Kaka had signed up to go to China with a group. He had been wanting to go to China for ages and the opportunity came up to go on an organised trip and he grabbed it. It was a whistle stop tour of the main places but that was the sort of trip he enjoyed. Been there, done that; he also enjoyed meeting new people. Usually on such trips, he went with Keshubhai. Both enjoyed travelling and seeing new places they could tick off their list! But at the time Keshubhai was a little poorly and was not able to go. Undeterred, Kaka travelled without him and had a wonderful time. He loved China and as it was just before the Olympics there was a lot of construction going on.

In September 2008, we had my cousin Ansuya's sons, Raju and Ricky's weddings in Mombasa and Dar es Salaam (Dar). Hitesh had been wanting to climb Kilimanjaro for some time now so this seemed an ideal opportunity to combine a holiday with a wedding. We decided to join him later for a safari so Nikhil and I and Bena's girls (Bhavini and Aasha) were going to join him in Tanzania after his climb. Bena and Vipul were coming straight to Mombasa. Arjun still had school and was therefore going to be 'home alone'.

Kaka was excited that we were all going and decided he would also make the trip to Kenya and Tanzania. He wanted to make the trip for other reasons too. His first cousin, Raishikaka had been recently diagnosed with stomach cancer in Kenya and Kaka wanted to go and visit his cousin for what he felt would probably be the last time.

Raishikaka had also been in Fort Hall and they had had a close relationship; with the passing of time, a lot of other relations such as Kaka's brother had passed away and so Raishikaka was one of his closest relatives outside our extended family.

Also, Kaka's friend Kapoorbhai's wife Santaben had been fasting for 108 days and after *paryushan*, when the fasting ended, a big celebration with a *jamvanu* was planned at the *mahajanwadi* in Nairobi. Kaka had already received an invitation for this and thought this was the ideal opportunity to meet everyone, so he planned his trip around these events as well. He was going to Nairobi to initially meet Raishikaka and to attend the dinner and then after about 10 days in Nairobi, we would fly to Mombasa together for the wedding and then go to Dar for the 2nd

wedding with a trip to Zanzibar during our stay in Dar and then fly out from Dar back to the UK. It promised to be another exciting trip. Ba was adamant she did not want to come

It was after China that Kaka started to lose his appetite and lose weight. Initially the weight loss was viewed favourably by all of us. Kaka was pleased he had managed to cut down on his food intake and had lost about a stone. He was still going shopping regularly and nothing seemed amiss. However he was complaining about his loss of appetite and his legs seemed to be hurting him.

We were all busy planning for our trip and did not take any of Kaka's health issues seriously. Hitesh flew out a week ahead of us, and then we (Nikhil, Bhavini, Aasha and I) flew out just at the start of *paryushan*. Ba was planning to do a *navai* but we were not going to be there for the celebration and even Kaka was not there for the breaking of the fast having flown straight after the end of *Paryushan*.

We found out later, that Kaka had been quite poorly the last few weeks before he flew out to the point of him thinking about cancelling the trip. His frequent visits to the doctor only resulted in trying out different medications all to no avail. But his heart was set on coming to Kenya and so somehow he must have willed himself better. When he landed we were still in Tanzania on safari. He stayed initially with Raishikaka and then stayed with another friend of his from Fort Hall.

By the time we met up with him, the big celebration to mark the ending of Santaben's 108 day fast had also taken place. He was thrilled to have been present for this wonderful occasion and reproached us for not being there. He had met up with so many people that he had not seen for a very long time and everyone had been asking about us especially Santaben's family who wanted us all to come for lunch at their house so he had decided to accept on our behalf! We only had a couple of days in Nairobi before flying off to Mombasa so none of us were too thrilled about going for lunch especially as we had also arranged for a driver to take us to Fort Hall but we acquiesced and so all of us including Nikhil, Aasha and Bhavini went for lunch there. It was good to meet with Santaben's children.

We set off early morning to go to Fort Hall, or Muranga as it is now known. It is around 50 miles from Nairobi and whilst the roads have improved considerably, the traffic is horrendous especially as there are a lot of industries on the way. Still it did not take us too long and soon we were in Fort Hall, but it had changed beyond recognition. As I recalled, previously, the entrance to the town was a small petrol station, after which you went up this short road at the top of which was a small roundabout. A few houses before the roundabout was our house; at the top of the roundabout, one of the corner houses was Bapuji and Amritba's house. If you carried on straight up you would come to the police station and some fields where we used to go on our daily walk as we brushed our teeth with *dattan*.

Now as we entered the town, it was like a thriving marketplace. There were little shops and stalls everywhere and so many people! All the big shops seemed to be owned by Benson Mogo; his name was everywhere. He was the gentleman who had bought our house and shop in 1970, paid the full price without haggling and let us stay in the house rent free until we moved to the UK in 1971. Kaka had been to visit him before. Hitesh and I had also come to visit Fort Hall in 1985, but we had not met up with him then. The kids were all curious to meet up with him especially as he seemed to be such a big shot in the town! Kaka had managed to contact him that we were coming so he was expecting us. And what a welcome he and his wife gave us.

Kaka, Benson, his wife, me, Hitesh, Bhavini and Aasha in Fort Hall at our old house.

They gave us a tour of the house; the house that I had grown up in. They had extended it adding another room on top. They wanted us to stay for the night and were disappointed that we could not even stay for lunch! Both he and his wife had taken a particular shine to Bhavini and were so happy to meet all of us. He said to Hitesh what a lucky man he was to have Kaka as a father in law. He said Kaka was a wonderful man and true gentleman and that he owed his business success to buying his first shop from us. Now he practically owned the town! Kaka had always been equally complimentary of him. He was a straight forward businessman. It was a particularly touching moment when they embraced each other. All barriers of race, colour, and creed were put to one side; it was just 2 human beings connecting!

Unfortunately as we were on a tight schedule, we had to take our leave all too quickly. Kaka also wanted to go and visit our family doctor's wife who lived alone and whose son had recently passed away. She lived about 5 minutes away from the main town. The door was padlocked but when we knocked repeatedly one of the servants came out and we were let in. She was an invalid and in bed but in going to see her, Kaka provided her with a moment's solace, that she was not totally forgotten! We would not bother, if we had not had any sort of contact for the best part of 40 years. It may sound harsh, but we were relieved when we found the gate padlocked. But Kaka persevered and kept knocking till he finally got an answer. When we saw the state she was in, we were once more quite embarrassed to intrude upon the privacy of a frail woman lying in bed. She had difficulty remembering and it took a while for Kaka to get across who he was. But again he persevered and then she was actually in tears that someone from the old days had come to visit her. Kaka passed on his condolences with regards to her son who had recently passed away. She had not seen him for years as he lived in Mombasa and never made the effort to visit. But Kaka had made the effort. He had remembered and for a brief moment, he had lit up her life. It was these types of gestures, the human interactions that made both my parents so special. They persevered when we would have given up.

After this we went back to Nairobi and Kapoorbhai's for lunch, following which Kaka had wanted us to visit Raishikaka. He was looking quite frail but mentally very alert and was really thrilled to see us. The next day we were due to fly out to Mombasa. At the airport we met up with Dinuben and Rasikbanevi, as well as Zavbhai and Kanchanbhabhi who were also travelling to Mombasa for the wedding.

That night we had a dinner organised by a distant cousin and from the next day the festivities were due to start. It was really hot in Mombasa and the cottages were lovely with a pool to cool us down but alas we were tied up due to lunches and dinners organised on a daily basis. So from early morning we would go to Ansuya's house to help with all the food preparation and setting up; there was so much to do!

The day after we arrived on 10th September, we were all in the garden, the ladies chopping vegetables and helping with other chores, and the men setting up; suddenly Rasikbanevi fainted. He immediately got up and we thought it was just sunstroke and told him to stay in the shade. Then a few minutes later, he fainted again. Immediately an ambulance was called and Hitesh performed CPR on him. He was breathing but unconscious. Not the perfect start to all the festivities and everyone was praying that he would recover. The ambulance took its time due to the traffic and he was taken to hospital in town over an hour away. He was kept in ICU and rehydrated intravenously but luckily it was nothing too serious. He was dehydrated and lacking in sodium and was released after a couple of days. Kaka on the other hand, who in London had been suffering from poor appetite and pain in his legs seemed to be fine.

The next few days consisted of lunches and dinners, some of them themed nights. We had a Swahili night, a Hawaiian night, *raas*[95] *garba*; sounds like fun but by Saturday, the day of Ricky and Meera's wedding, we were exhausted. The temperatures were in the mid-30s, not ideal for dressing up in all your finery. The wedding on Saturday was at a beach but in the afternoon so we were all suffering in the midday heat; I'm not sure how they managed to sit with all their attire in front of the sacred fire as well! A pool party would have been much more fun!

The rich food we had been eating for lunch and dinners was taking its toll and all of us, including Kaka were suffering from stomach upsets. At least that's what we assumed in Kaka's case too. We had been invited to lunch on the Monday at a relation's house and although Kaka was feeling a little poorly, he wanted to come along. At the lunch, he barely ate a *rotli* and threw up a bit. They had wanted to take us sightseeing, but as he was not feeling too well, some of us decided to come back early to the cottages.

We were just walking from the cottage reception to our cottage when all of a sudden he threw up again on the steps. The vomit was very black and the manager came rushing out from reception. He looked very concerned. He kept shaking his head and saying this was not good and immediately called a doctor. We managed to get him slowly back to the cottage and change. The doctor came and prescribed some tablets and

---

[95] Gujarati folk dance involving sticks

told us to get an endoscopy done when we were back in the UK. After about an hour, Kaka was feeling slightly better and Hitesh made a cup of tea. As Kaka got up from the bed to come to the table, he suddenly collapsed without warning! He just lay on the floor, unconscious, despite us trying to wake him. Hitesh slapped him a few times on the cheek to no avail. I was so worried that I kept reciting the *navkar mantra* and pleading for him not be taken away yet, not here, not during the festivities. And then, miracle of miracles, after what seemed an eternity but probably was about 10 minutes, he gained consciousness. We were ecstatic. He felt ok and had tea and biscuits and his medication.

After this he felt fine. The next few days, he took it easy, but on Friday, we had a long journey to Dar. Bena was all for returning to the UK with Kaka but Kaka was equally adamant that he wanted to go to Dar. So on Wednesday, we decided to go to the doctor and confirm that he, as well as Raskibanevi, (who had been fine after his initial stay in hospital) were both ok to make the trip. The doctor confirmed that both Kaka and Rasikbanevi were fine. Kaka looked ok and was very keen to come, so we decided not to change any plans. It was a long 10 hour coach trip to Dar but both of them coped admirably.

In Tanzania, we were also joined by Pradipbhai from India who had accompanied Kaka to Australia the year before. Kaka seemed to be getting back to his old self, but his appetite had decreased.

All the festivities in Dar – *raas garba* and dinners and the wedding were organised really well. The day after the wedding, Bena, Vipul, Hitesh and I along with Kaka had organised to go to Zanzibar for a few days. After this the plan was to come back to Dar and fly out from Dar. We took a ferry to Zanzibar; the sea was rough and the ferry ride was hair raising to say the least. Zanzibar was beautiful, a veritable paradise in the middle of the Indian Ocean.

We stayed in the old town, a place that seemed to have been forgotten by time. It was full of cobbled streets and narrow alley ways. Our hotel was so beautiful, it looked like a sultan's palace. We took a tour of the spice plantations and mangroves and relaxed in this beautiful paradise. We also went for a bit of sightseeing around the island to see the sultan's palace; Kaka did not join us for this. Instead, he and Bena played cards. We had only managed to find one Indian vegetarian restaurant in the old town. We ate here for at least one meal so Kaka could have one decent meal but it was not a great restaurant and Kaka's appetite was not improving. But otherwise he seemed fine.

After a few days of relaxing and enjoying the sun and the sea, it was time to head back to London. Our flight was leaving from Dar in the night, so we took a morning ferry back from Zanzibar, arriving in Dar a few hours later. Raju's in laws had already arranged for us to have lunch at their place. It was so good to have lovely home cooked food again and even Kaka managed to eat more than the last few days.

We had left some of our bags at the hotel that we had been staying at previously so went to pick these up before going to the airport to take the flight back home. We had been away a long time. Hitesh, five weeks, Kaka and myself 4 weeks. Arjun had been home alone for at least 3 of these weeks. Nikhil, Bhavini and Aasha had not come to Tanzania for Raju's wedding and had flown back from Mombasa. As we touched down in London, Kaka seemed to be his old self. He started getting his bag from the cabin above and was keen on getting home. We had organised a cab to take us back to Harrow, but he was happy to go to Ilford on the train. He even took his suitcase with him!

Home again, more drama and sorrow

During our absence, the world had turned upside down! At least the financial world had! Lehman Brothers, a huge American bank had collapsed on 15 September 2008, leading to shock waves in the industry. All the banks were wondering who would be next and no one wanted to lend any more money to each other, leading to financial chaos.

The share prices of all the banks plummeted. I could only watch helplessly as my huge portfolio of RBS shares crashed in value. From a high of around £6 in July, they touched £1 in October and then the question was do you sell now, or hang on and hope this is just a temporary blip. Kaka was quite philosophical about it all. What is the point of dwelling on it, he said. What has happened, has happened. Forget about it, he said.

Anyway there were much more important matters to think about. We thought that Kaka would become his old self as he returned home but that was not the case. After a few days, he complained again about not being able to eat. Still the doctor did not immediately refer him to a consultant but changed his medication. I had said to Manjula to mention that he had collapsed in Kenya and thrown up and that they had suggested he have an endoscopy but the doctor did not want to do this. The change of medication did nothing and eventually both Shailesh and Manjula went to see the doctor; by this time, Kaka had lost around 4 stones. Finally the doctor agreed for Kaka to be referred to a consultant.

When the consultant saw Kaka, he was shocked to see how emaciated he had become within the space of 6 months. Shailesh had taken pictures so this could be demonstrated graphically. After the tests were done, it was clear that Kaka had stomach cancer. The consultant cancelled his other appointments to perform an emergency operation. Whilst the operation was successful, the cancer had spread and so we were on borrowed time. At first, this was not obvious to us. Kaka seemed to have improved, the operation was successful and so we were under the impression that when he recovered more and regained his strength, he would be undergoing chemotherapy. After a few weeks in hospital, Kaka was able to come home the week before Christmas. We had decided to keep a *bhajan* and *bhojan*[96] on Christmas Eve with the whole extended family, so over 50 people. Kaka and Ba loved these gatherings.

We had requested for each family to select a *bhajan* that they wanted to sing; Kaka chose 2 and he also recited the *kshamapana*[97] at the end. Dilip had recorded the whole *bhajan* session so we still play Kaka reciting the *kshamapana*. It feels like he is there in person!

During the Christmas holidays, Kaka's spirits had been lifted by having the whole family around him. Come January and everyone was back at work, the weather was pretty gloomy and wet so it was no surprise that during January and February he became weaker and unable to do much. We used to visit at least on a weekly basis and he perked up during these times. He rested a lot but mentally he was completely alert and started getting his affairs in order. He used to say you should always be prepared After the Christmas holidays, round about the end of January, we were told by the consultant that the cancer had spread and chemotherapy was not an option. We were all devastated with the news. Although he was 81, Kaka had always been strong, walking a few miles a day, bringing me shopping, so we thought he would be able to overcome any disease.

But Kaka was philosophical. Everyone has to go one day he reminded us, you just have to be prepared. And we had been given that time. But to watch someone deteriorate slowly is agonising to watch, you are completely helpless. To try and overcome that feeling of helplessness, we did what we could. Initially Kaka was still trying to recover; he would eat a little and continued with the shopping. But soon it was

---

[96] Meal

[97] Jain forgiveness prayer usually recited at the end of a *bhajan* session

becoming too much for him and his strength was failing him. But he was not one to give up so easily.

So we kept up our normal routine and went about our business, but visited him a little more frequently, which of course they were overjoyed about. We started giving him fresh juices daily, including wheatgrass juice which we grew at home. The brunt of the responsibility feel upon Ba who became busier than normal. We would all help when we could and Bena often stayed there to help out and Niru came over from the US.

In March, he was doing reasonably well and so Bena had booked a trip to India in May, Manjula a trip to Alaska at the end of May, and I booked a trip to Sri Lanka for mid-June. I asked him whether he wanted to come along. Normally, he would have jumped at the chance. 'Let me get better first' he said. Perhaps that should have alerted me. Instead I saw his illness as a temporary blip and expected him to bounce back. After all this was Kaka, my father who had always been strong, who had survived a horrific car accident and come out unscathed even though he had lost so much blood and had no blood transfusion. And it looked as if our hopes of Kaka getting better were becoming a reality. When we had a celebration for Arjun's 18th birthday and Hitesh's 50th birthday in a small hall, Kaka came to this and was walking unaided, and able to eat. He seemed fine, if a little weak. A few weeks later, he also went to Dilip's for Paras's 21st birthday but he was weaker at that time, although he did feed Paras some birthday cake.

Maybe the juice therapy helped, or maybe it prolonged the inevitable, but he was deteriorating fast. By the end of April he was a shadow of his former self. Barely able to perform his daily routine by himself, he now had carers visiting him and helping him with showering and going to the toilet. The McMillan nurses had started visiting to try and make his stay more comfortable. Virtually everything he ate, he would throw up. By May he'd become virtually bed bound. Unable even to take in any water, he'd become withered. Despairing as to what to do, we eventually got him admitted to hospital as an emergency case. The doctors were shocked at how dehydrated he was and administered saline and glucose drips round the clock. For the first couple of days, he looked radiant again, he could speak as he was not so hoarse. Niru paid a surprise visit and he was really happy to see her. So we all perked up and thought he was on the road to recovery. But alas! Our euphoria was short lived and he started throwing up again and unable to eat. After about 10 days in hospital he was released again as there was nothing further they could do. And so it was that essentially he was brought back home to die peacefully in a familiar environment.

His rapid deterioration of health was a shock to everyone but we had so many people rallying around to help. He had so many visitors and so many phone calls on a daily basis. All of us stayed over when we could to assist and spend time with him and even my cousins came from Kenya and India to visit him. All of this showed us, if we didn't know it already, how popular and charismatic a figure he was and that he was going to be sorely missed. Nikhil and Arjun had also been coming regularly to visit their beloved grandfather and he would still ask them about their studies and sports. All the grandchildren found it particularly distressing to watch him deteriorate.

I remember in the last week he looked like he was eating something from his hand. I asked him what he was doing and he replied he was eating some raisins. His hand was empty. It was heart breaking. The dehydration and fasting were making him hallucinate and he was mixing dreams and reality. On Sunday before he passed away, I had stayed over. It was just me and Ba, Bena having gone back home. In the middle of the night, I heard Ba shouting. I woke up to find that Kaka's sheets were wet. He had no strength any more to get out of bed. Between me and Ba, we could not move him to change the sheets. All we could do was lift him enough to put some dry sheets underneath. I felt utterly helpless. It is a memory that keeps haunting me. The next day, they inserted a catheter.

Manjula and Mahesh came back from their Alaska trip on Monday and she was eagerly showing him the photos but he was not interested. He even got to meet the latest addition to our family, Jainam, Niru's grandson. We felt Kaka had been hanging on, until we were all there. He passed away 3 days after Niru and family arrived from the States. The last time he spoke was on the Tuesday, when Niru and family arrived. He was barely able to talk but just before they all arrived, he had a phone call from Raishikaka, his cousin who had been diagnosed with cancer the year before and who Kaka had gone to visit only last year. It was ironic that Raishikaka, was recovering from his stomach cancer and Kaka who at the time did not even know he also had stomach cancer, was now at his deathbed.

Raishikaka was giving Kaka advice – not to lose hope and to take everything in your stride. It was fitting that the last call he took was from someone who he'd known his whole life, someone who was so close to him despite the distance that separated them.

On Wednesday, Kaka was barely able to breathe and an oxygen tank was delivered to us, but with no guidance as to operation, we could not use it. Instead we resorted to chanting mantras and singing *bhajans* around his bedside knowing the end was imminent.

Kaka passed away on early Friday morning around 5am on 5 June. We had been going to see him in the evenings and also when time allowed, I used to visit him at lunchtimes briefly. As these times lots of other people were around too, I had said to Manjula that I would go there first thing before I went to work. As I was about to leave on Friday morning, Manjula phoned and said it was not going to possible as she felt Kaka had departed already. We had been preparing for this day and in some ways were wanting for his pain to be over, but when it finally came, it was still too sudden. We wished for a few more days, hours, moments!

It was eerily quiet for a little while when we all got there in the early morning but then everything was bustling again as arrangements for the *sadadi* and funeral were being discussed. Monica and Jainam were due to fly out on the Sunday 7 June, so the *sadadi* was arranged for the same day, Friday evening and provisionally the funeral was arranged for Saturday morning. However as he had died at home, obtaining a death certificate was another challenge; the GP didn't turn up until the afternoon, so it was touch and go as to whether the funeral would take place on Saturday at 9am.

None of the grandchildren needed to be prompted to say something at the *sadadi* or funeral. They all wanted to express their deep respect and admiration for him. Hinesh summed it up when he said that 'Kaka was the perfect gentleman.'

2 weeks after Kaka passed away, we went to Sri Lanka. The trip had been organised in March when Kaka had been looking like he was improving. Mentally we had decided that we would not go if Kaka was still around but since it had been 2 weeks since his death, and all the final rites had been concluded, we went ahead. Sri Lanka is a beautiful place and we had a relaxing holiday but all my thoughts revolved around Kaka. We had taken lots of Kaka's clothes to distribute there and 2 days after we got there it was Father's day. So it was a good day to do this act of charity. We also took some more clothes with us when we toured the island and gave them to grateful locals. It was an emotional time, so soon after Kaka's death but the holiday gave us time to reflect on him and also a chance to recommence writing my biography about my parents again. Once he had been diagnosed with cancer, Kaka had told me that I should finish this before he passed away but somehow I had no inclination whatsoever. My regret is that he never saw or read what I had already

written. More than 6 years after Kaka passed away, I'm still trying to finish this.

And so it was that Ba was now without her companion of 63 years. The last year had been extremely busy for her as she had to take care of his needs, had to look after all the visitors that came to visit him, and had to answer all the hundreds of phone calls we received daily. Although we were all there to assist, she had borne the brunt of the work.

Now suddenly she was out of a job! The house that had been bustling with life the last year was suddenly silent. It had been like a party atmosphere, with visitors dropping in to provide solace to Kaka briefly but then staying for a chat or food or daily *bhajans*. Now the visitors had dried up, the phone barely rang. It was back to normality for everyone. Everyone that is except Ba, who had to come to terms with a difficult chapter in her life – living without her life partner of over 60 years.

And then she had another blow; 6 weeks after Kaka passed away, we heard that my Veljimama, her brother had also passed away in Mumbai. Ba now only had one sibling left, Dahimasi who lived in Jamnagar. But my mum, barely 5ft was a very strong lady. All her life she had had setbacks and these were yet more setbacks. She soldiered on. And still she suffered setbacks. In February 2010, my cousin Gulab's wife Pannabhabhi who had also been diagnosed with cancer passed away. In August 2010, Ba lost Dahimasi. The last remaining out of her brothers and sisters, Ba carried on bravely for the remainder of her time on this earth.

Ba's remaining years

When Kaka was in hospital, Ba had decided that she was not going to move out of the family home upon his death. She did not want to be uprooted in her twilight years. Whilst initially we had tried to dissuade her of this, her mind was made up. As I get older and more set in my ways, I can now comprehend her decision. Slowly by slowly, apart from the immediate family, the visitors dried up, the phone stopped ringing, there was only one person to cook for and she didn't feel like cooking or eating most of the time. In truth, Kaka's death had sucked the life out of her too.

She was, however, a determined lady. The phone calls had stopped; so she started calling everyone, in much the same way that Kaka had done regularly before he became ill. Hers were brief to the point calls and sometimes she left you hanging mid-sentence as she had conveyed her message and did not wait to hear your response! She also took to buying fruits and vegetables to give to people when they came round. She could not go to the market so she took to going to the corner shop and then if she bought more than she could carry, she would get one of the staff to bring it home!

Shailesh, Manjula would visit 3-4 times a week and my cousins would come over regularly. Bena and I would usually visit once a week. Niru also came over frequently and stayed for a month or even longer. But it was a lonely existence especially in winter. She had never ventured out much and she was unfamiliar with the transport system so there was no way she could come to my house or Bena's house on her own.

Those who lived in Ilford would take it in turns to drop in daily so at least she would see someone if only briefly. Manjula also organised yoga classes at the house so everyone would see her on a weekly basis and she could also partake in those classes.

As the boys were now both at university, I decided to spend a couple of nights a week at the Mayfair house too. Hitesh was busy coaching badminton in the evenings on Mondays and Tuesdays so I decided I would come there on those days and go to work from there. It was no sacrifice on my part. I got a ready cooked meal and was pampered, but she was always so thrilled to see me. She really looked forward to those days. We would usually watch some religious programme together, converse for a short period and then she would continue reading her book. She seemed to read the same pages over and over again. I was never quite sure why that was. I did try and ask her but she smiled and said it was not the same pages.

On the days that I did not go to see her, she would phone almost as I opened the door. She had this uncanny ability to know that I would be returning back from work. And then she would ask the obvious, 'so you've come back from work?' I was usually tired and not in the mood for pointless conversations so I would respond with one word answers and within a minute she would ring off. What I would give now for the phone to ring just one more time and have one of those pointless conversations! They say you never really appreciate what you have until you lose it. It was like that with my mum. She was a rough diamond whose true worth we only realised after she had passed away.

Niru had come over for the last 3 months and she had been staying with Ba. As a result, I had recently stopped my weekly visits but we still used to go and see her the weekends on a regular basis.

In February, Ba had been persuaded to come and stay with Bena for 10 days and Bena had taken her round to visit all the relations that lived in this area. She had even come over to my house for a farewell party I had organised for Nikhil who was going off on his travels.

We had taken her to the Hare Krishna *mandir*[98] in Watford and on the day that Bena dropped her back, they had stopped off at *Oshwal* centre for the inaugural elderly people's lunch. You could sponsor these events and unbeknown to Bena, Ba had gone to the office and told them that she was sponsoring the event that day. They already had a sponsor, but she persuaded the other sponsor to step aside this time so she could sponsor as she said she was not sure when she would get this opportunity again. Bena only found out when they made the announcement of the sponsor!

In March, Niru finally went back after 3 months and Bena had taken a trip to South America. We had just returned from a week's skiing holiday. The following week Ba had been feeling a little unwell; she was doing her *ayambil* fasting but from Wednesday had been complaining of a pain in the stomach and saying she had had a stroke. She didn't sound like she had a stroke. She was coherent and mobile and due to her *ayambil*, did not want to go to the doctor or hospital. On Friday, I went to visit and whilst she looked frail, she was happy to see me. It only dawns on you when you go to visit, how lonely her life had been since my dad passed away and that basically she was waiting to die. I told her that it was no sin to break her *ayambil* but she was adamant on finishing it. It was the last day.

Ayambils had always been really important to her. For years, she would host the *ayambils*, which lasted 9 days, at her house, cooking for 10-15 people all sorts of varieties of *ayambil* foods, even though she would only eat one thing. It was only recently that she had not been able to host these.

That day she was tired and after lunch, she said she'd lie down for a while. After she drifted off to sleep, I left. This was the last time that I saw her. I phoned her the following day, Saturday. She was still feeling unwell and Manjula had already phoned for an ambulance and was on her way to Ba. Shailesh was also on his way.

She was taken to hospital and apparently the signs were not good. She had suffered a massive heart attack, probably on the Wednesday when she believed that she'd had a stroke.

---

[98] Hindu temple

I did intend to visit her in hospital but as she had not been assigned a ward, I decided to wait until that had been done and by then it was getting to be evening time. I thought I'd see her early the next morning and we were on our way to the hospital early on Sunday morning but we got a message that she had passed away around 8am. It was Sunday April 8. Some things are not meant to be.

But what a way to go. She had finished her *ayambil* which was so important to her. She had also on her visit to Bena, attended the elderly function at *Oshwal* centre which on the spur of the moment she decided to sponsor the lunch for, saying she was not sure she would get that opportunity again. And she was right. Also she had pledged a donation for the Navagam reunion due to take place later in the year and I had taken her the cheque when I went to visit on Friday. So whilst she had passed away before this event took place, her good work was carrying on without her.

At the hospital, she must have caused quite a stir as a result of being so coherent and mobile despite having suffered a massive heart attack. Manjula said quite a few doctors came to visit this petite lady who seemed to have defied medical science! Others mentioned that she kept looking up and saying they were coming for her as if she knew the end was nigh.

On Sunday, she looked quite peaceful and serene in the hospital. I'm sure she's in a happier place. The hardest was to break the news to Bena who was on a trip to South America. Bena had seen Ba a couple of weeks ago and for her it was totally unexpected. Ba's death has hit us a lot harder than expected. Maybe it was the finality of it all, the end of an era, the end of a generation.

Everyone we meet still mentions how she would always phone them regularly. Since Kaka had passed away, she had taken on this role of keeping in touch with everyone and passing on the news. We miss that and miss her, more than we thought we would.

When we went to visit, conversations were limited and short as she did not have many interests and we were unable to converse fluently with her, but she was always in the background. We had lost someone special. It was an uncomfortable feeling that someone who has your best interests at heart, who loves you unconditionally no matter what, and who you could pick up the phone to anytime, is no longer there. For the rest of my life, I will cherish the fond memories of our time together, especially as I got to know her better as a result of this project.

Lest we forget

I initially started this project to document my parents' remarkable history for future generations. Not that it is unique; it is a similar story for a lot of East African Asians, but I did not want my children or their children to forget their roots. I wanted them all to remember the sacrifices their ancestors had made to ensure their children had a better and easier life than they had. However in embarking upon this project, I learnt so much about my parents' characters. I learnt so much about their history, I learnt so much about their principles, family values and the respect they had for their elders, I learnt so much about friendship and helping each other and most of all, I learnt so much about the sacrifices they made for us and the unconditional love they bestowed upon us.

All of us should be grateful for the courageous step they took in venturing out to Kenya. We, our children or our grandchildren will never know what it is like to be hungry and not get one decent meal a day. We see images of poor and hungry children and I think, we could have been caught up in that spiral, were it not for the fact that they took the courage to venture into the unknown.

Because of the emphasis they placed upon education, they were willing to send their children abroad to study, and remarkably within one generation, the illiterate parents had university educated children. They who had never set foot outside of India, took the bold step of settling first in Kenya and then England. Amidst all this change, they held on to their principles, their religion, their values and they remained true to themselves.

We have now become rich; we have become highly educated; we go on holidays around the globe; through the internet, we can communicate instantly to anyone around the world. But our wealth and material possessions, have made us increasingly possessive and selfish; our education has made us more prejudiced and snobbish; our globetrotting has made us superior spectators; our instant communication has stopped us connecting meaningfully with our fellow human beings. I'm not saying that we should not be progressing, but let us stop and consider what it is that we are striving for. Let us try and share our wealth more equally; let us try and use our education to serve humanity; let us try and become ethical travellers; let us spend quality time with our parents, friends and children. I hope that this book will awaken those values in us that our parents held dear and that it will help remind us of our roots lest we forget.

Kaka and Ba's legacy

Kaka date of birth 25/08/1927
Date of death 05/06/2009

Ba date of birth 01/01/1930
Date of death 08/04/2012

A couple of years ago, Manjula, Bena and I, along with our respective husbands, went to visit Savarkundla, a school in Gujarat for slum children. The children aged between 6-8, were very curious and eager to learn. We, the VIPs, were introduced as coming from a land far, far away in an aeroplane, an object that they would have seen flying in the skies but never been on. More than 40 children were all squashed together on the floor in a small area. Seeing these children, I imagined the kind of schooling Kaka and Ba would have received and how wide eyed and curious they might have been. At that age, they had probably never even heard of Kenya or England, let alone envisaged they would live there one day. Even in their wildest dreams, they could not have dreamt of the life they were destined to lead: their hard work would end their financial worries and they would be well off; they would be able to educate their children and give them a head start in life; they would be able to travel to so many countries and see the world; they would meet some wonderful people on the way and light up so many people's lives. Amidst all this change, their religion and culture kept them anchored to their roots.

For Kaka and Ba, their family was their pride and joy. 11 months after Kaka passed away, and a few months after Pannabhabhi passed away, Manan, Gulab and Pannabhabhi's son got married.

Since Ba passed away, Kavita has got married as well as Dilip's 3 children, Khilna, Hinesh and Paras. Bena's daughter Aasha recently got engaged. Whilst missing those who have departed, these occasions have been fantastic get togethers for the extended family. Hinesh's wedding in India was an opportune occasion for my cousins in India and their families to attend and meet us and our children. A lot of these cousins and 2nd cousins now keep in touch on whatsapp and facebook and meet regularly.

2 years ago, Zavbhai also passed away, having suffered from dementia over the last few years.

Shailesh hosts a *bhajan* session annually in memory of not just Kaka and Ba but all our loved ones who have now departed. Kaka and Ba would be proud to learn that these occasions are celebrated and that everyone makes a great effort to attend.

Kaka and Ba would be happy to hear that even though they have left us, their spirit lives on in their children and grandchildren who have all inherited something special from Kaka and Ba, whether it be love for travelling, singing, playing cards, socialising, helping others, cooking, spirituality, or determination.

Kaka and Ba's grandchildren along with other cousins at Paras and Reena's wedding

Niru's Family

Back left to right Monica, Raju and Meena; front left to right Jainam, Manu, Niru and Devika

Niru, the eldest daughter is 68, and is married to Manu. She lives in the Washington DC area in USA. Now retired, she worked as an accountant. They have 2 children, Raju and Meena. Niru enjoys sewing, gardening and travelling.

Raju is married to Monica and lives near his parents. Raju works as an electrical engineer in the US, but spent 5 years working in the UK. They have 2 children, Jainam, 7 and Devika, 5. The children both attend Jain classes on Sundays.

Meena is a product manager in San Francisco. She enjoys sailing, camping and skiing.

Manjula's family

Mahesh, Vijay, Kavita, Uttam and Manjula

Vijay in Baffin Island

Kavita, Jasmine and James

Jasmine and Uttam

Manjula, the second daughter is 63 and married to Mahesh. She lives in Ilford and is a trained holistic therapist and has 3 children, Uttam, Vijay and Kavita. Manjula enjoys travelling and gardening.

Uttam works as a DJ and is a music producer on a global level. He currently resides in Los Angeles.

Vijay works as an aeronautics engineer in Bristol. He has a passion for adventure and was part of the first British team to cross the Penny ice cap on Baffin Island in the Canadian Arctic.

Kavita is married to James and lives in Manchester. They have a daughter Jasmine, who shares her birthday with her mum.

Bena's family

Vipul, Aasha, Bhavini and Bena

Prafula (Bena) the third daughter is 61 and married to Vipul. She lives in Harrow and has 2 daughters, Bhavini and Aasha. She enjoys travelling and has recently organised trips for groups to China, Nepal and South America

Bhavini and Aasha both work in the City and are actively involved in Shishukunj, a charitable organisation run by the youth for the youth, instilling moral values in children aged 5 upwards to become responsible citizens. Aasha has recently become engaged to Sunil.

My family

Nikhil, Hitesh, me and Arjun

I am Kaka and Ba's fourth daughter, 55 and married to Hitesh. I live in Harrow, 5 minutes from Bena and have 2 sons, Nikhil and Arjun. An accountant by profession, I recently retired after 33 years of working in the City and have been on a mission since then to finish this book. I enjoy travelling, skiing, reading and writing.

Nikhil and Arjun both work in the financial sector in Canary Wharf and are keen sportsmen, playing football and squash regularly. They love travelling, and going on skiing and diving holidays.

Shailesh's family

Priya, Shailesh, Sachin, Alpa and Anjali

Shailesh, the only son is 53 and married to Alpa. He lives in Ilford, about 15 minutes from Ba and Kaka's house. He has 3 children, Sachin, Priya and Anjali. He works in the city as a computer programmer. He enjoys travelling and playing tennis.

Sachin is currently at university studying computing and mobile app design. He enjoys martial arts, badminton and travelling.

Priya is also currently at university and studying economics and business management. She enjoys socialising, meeting friends and badminton.

Anjali is still a teenager and at school. She enjoys making and decorating cakes and playing badminton.

Bapuji and Amritba's legacy

Zavbhai passed away in 2013. He was married to Kanchanbhabhi. They have 2 sons, Raju and Sanjay.

Raju is married to Ansuiya and their children are Nitish and Phoolna.

Sanjay is married to Bindi and their children are Jaini and Reyen.

Dinuben is married to Rasikbanevi and they have 2 children, Samir and Meena.

Samir is married to Rashmi and their children are Viraj and Riya.

Gulab was married to Pannabhabhi who passed away in 2010. They have 2 sons, Chetan and Manan.

Chetan is married to Tejal and their children are Aditya and Arushi.

Manan is married to Sapna.

Ansuya is married to Jayant and they have 3 children, Raju, Seiya and Ricky.

Raju is married to Arti and their children are Kian and Sky.

Seiya is married to Birju and their children are Parissa and Savan.

Ricky is married to Meera and their son is Kai.

Sunita is married to Shanti and they have 2 children, Vijal and Anna.

Dilip is married to Nilam and they have 3 children, Khilna, Hinesh and Paras.

Khilna is married to Rupen.

Hinesh is married to Shuchi.

Paras is married to Reena.

Kavita and James's wedding with both sets of parents

Sanjay, Jaini, Khilna, Reyen, Bindi and Rupen at Hinesh's wedding in India

Naman, his wife Rupal, Samyak, Dhwani and her husband Mehul

With Dahimasi's grandson Vijal, his wife Rupal and daughter Dhriti

My cousins from India and their families at Hinesh and Shuchi's wedding

My cousins' children and their children at Paras and Reena's wedding

More cousins' children and their children at Paras and Reena's wedding

Some of my cousins and their families at Paras and Reena's wedding

Tributes

Tributes to Kaka upon his death 5 June 2009
Sadadi speeches

To Kaka, Our Beloved Father
I write this with a heavy heart
Losing you has torn our lives apart
You were the compass that guided us all the way
You were the trunk that supported us branches every day

You were the anchor that stopped our boat from drifting
You were the wings that kept us from falling
You were our sun that shone so bright
Now there is a darkness, we can't find the light

Where there were echoes of laughter once
We are now enveloped by a deathly silence
We miss your smile so warm and inviting
And all the fruit and vegetables shopping

You would not miss any family occasion
Arriving early to join in the celebration
Always ready to play *bhukh*ar or sing a *bhajan*
These simple pleasures gave you so much fun

Your life is a rags to riches story
But throughout it you retained your simplicity
You had a zest for life and loved travelling
Our holidays together were always so inspiring

Your kind and generous nature was remarkable
Your sheer hard work and courage admirable
You've helped so many in their time of need
No one will ever forget these great deeds

You told us to face every hardship with equanimity
Your last days were a testament to this philosophy
You bore every adversity with a smile
For you told us, this time too will pass in a while

We had still so many plans, so many dreams
Was it only yesterday, we talked about them it seems
Now we feel cold, empty inside and all alone
We've woken up and the dreams are all gone

To know and love you has been an honour, a privilege
You've taught us so much especially to have courage
How to laugh, love, smile and stand tall
And with you still watching, we know we won't fall

You will always be in our hearts and mind
And we know that if we search we will find
Signs of you everywhere so clear and bright
For what is death but the limit of our sight

You have left us a lifetime of memories
We will forever cherish each one of these
We've bared our souls to tell you all this
But most of all we pray that your soul is at peace

OM SHANTI SHANTI SHANTI From your loving Family
© Hasmita Shah 5 June 2009 (poem by me at Kaka's *sadadi*)

My dad – Hansraj Lakhamshi Shah

Thank you for all attending this very sad day marking the end of my Dad's present life, who sadly passed away early this morning aged 81, and beginning of his new life as his soul lives on. My dad was a very humble and simple man, highly respected by everyone that knew him. He had been instrumental in keeping harmony and peace with everyone around him. He had a certain kind of mystical aura around him that calmed any situation and you knew you could talk to him and he would always give correct guidance and you know your problems would disappear.

He never got cross with anyone and would ensure that others are happy before ensuring his own happiness. Even though, at times, he had very little money he would ensure the family did not go hungry and would sacrifice his own meals.

As you probably all know, my dad and his brother married my mum and her sister. My four sisters and I grew up alongside our cousins. My dad treated my cousins as his own children and gave them the same love and affection that he has given to my sisters and me. He had a unique quality of ensuring everyone was treated fairly and with respect and never said anything bad about anyone. Recently, he fulfilled his wish to visit many faraway places -San Francisco where he visited his granddaughter Meena, China, Kenya & Tanzania for Ricky and Raju's wedding, India, Dubai and Australia. He led a very active life and passionately cared for all. He would give so much love and happiness without asking for anything in return.

My dad fulfilled so much in his lifetime and touched so many hearts and, if in my lifetime, I can just achieve half of what he has achieved I would consider myself very gifted. Whatever I achieve I know my dad would be proud of me. He had my total respect and admiration for what he has achieved and what he has left behind. He was a guiding light to many of us and this will be sadly missed but we hope and pray his soul will find us and be reunited with us in some shape or form. He now has departed this life and his soul has been left assured that my mum (Ba) will be looked after and that he has nothing to worry.

Ba, on behalf of all my sisters and I, please take comfort in knowing that we will do our best together as a family to look after you and you have nothing to worry and nothing to fear.

Thank you for your time and patience in listening to me.
(Speech by Shailesh at Kaka's *sadadi*)

Speeches by the grandchildren at Kaka's *sadadi*

Our grandfather passed away when we were very young and Kaka has been like a grandfather to us our whole lives. One of the things I remember most vividly about Kaka is the sound of his voice when reciting '*kshamapna*' at *Pratikraman*. As young kids, *Pratikraman* used to seem like a chore however, when Kaka spoke the whole room echoed with his gentle yet powerful voice. Kaka also loved to play *bhukhar* and for many hours he would sit with myself and my cousins and keep us entertained.

Kaka has been an inspiration to us. His calm, dignified nature never faltered even when faced with the most emotional of situations. Never has anyone heard him raise his voice, nor has he ever let his smile fade away from his face. Kaka truly was a special man and for us younger males, symbolised the perfect gentleman.

Not how did he die, but how did he live
Not what did he gain, but what did he give
These are the units to measure the worth
Of a man as a man, regardless of birth

I hope we can all learn from the life Kaka led, and that his soul forever rests in peace.
(Speech by Hinesh)

Nana was one of the most selfless people I know. Even during his last few days, he would always ask how I was and how **MY** studies were going and he would motivate me to keep working hard and to make him proud. When someone said to me 'He was kaka to all of us', I think they summed up the admiration in which he was held by everyone.
(Speech by Aasha)

As many of you know, *Nana* was a man of the community. He gave a lot to the community and was loved and respected by many. He treated the community like his family and gave everything to it.
(Speech by Arjun)

An example of this was last year when we went on a family holiday to Kenya and we visited *Nana*'s old town and we saw his shop and the person who had bought his shop from him and who treated *Nana* as an old friend. After speaking to his friend we realised how much of an effect – a good effect he had on his family and his friends and it was amazing to see how much of an effect he still has these many years on.
(Speech by Nikhil)

Nana really liked travelling and he went to so many countries- he went to China, Australia, Kenya, USA, and Turkey in the last couple of years. He really wanted to go to Russia. My favourite memory of him was when we were little, he always kept *sakar*[99] in his pocket to give to us when we went to Ilford.
(Speech by Bhavini)

---

[99] Sugar cubes

Dada, you were full of peace and never hurt anyone. That is why I am so grateful to have you as my *Dada*. Wherever, you are now, I hope you are in a much better place as you deserve the best. *Dada*, I will always love you and will miss you very very much.
(Speech by Sachin)

I am very grateful you could all make it here today. My *Dada* was the best man in the whole world.
He loved and cared for everyone and he was always there when we needed him.
But now that he has gone, I am really, really sad, I just want him to come back.
I know that he will always be watching me and he will always be with me.
Dada, we will all miss you a lot and we will never forget what you have done for us.
Dada, we love you!
(Speech by Priya)

My *Dada* meant a lot to me and he worked so hard for all of us.
He wanted everyone to be happy and we all cared for him and will never forget him for as long as we all live. *Dada*, you will be sadly missed and we all love you very much.
(Speech by Anjali)

Raju's favourite activity with *Nana* is going fruit and vegetable shopping. They used to wake up around 6am every Saturday and spend the early part of their days together.
Nana has always been there for Raju since Raju's early childhood summers in England. Raju is extremely thankful for when *Nana* came to the US for our wedding, when he visited us in Leeds, and when he spent time with Raju when Raju was in the hospital. *Nana* has always been a kind hearted man. One funny example is when *Nani* taught me how to make *rotlis*. At first they came out like *khakras*[100] and Raju did not enjoy eating them. However, *Nana* did not mind and he appreciated my efforts despite the hardness.
(Speech by Monica, Raju's wife)

---

[100] Hard chapattis

Funeral speeches

Don't forget your parents. This was the advice given regularly to us by our parents. But how can we forget such a father. If we used to encounter any hardship, he would remind us that whatever happens, happens for the best. So what if he recently got cancer and was suffering – just think of how many people visited him as a result. Such was his welcoming attitude that every day we would receive so many guests at home and so many phoned him daily. And how lucky was Kaka in his final year to be able to visit Kenya once more and meet all his relations and his friends from when he was young. He even showed his grandchildren his old house and shop when they all visited Fort Hall.

Kaka you have always given us great advice and have brought us up to have good values. You have trusted us and given us freedom to fulfil all our aspirations. You have not studied a great deal but you wholeheartedly supported us to study as much as we wanted to. It is from observing your life that we are learning how to live a satisfied life. It is from observing your welcome that we are learning how to talk nicely to people and keep our tongues sweet. You have taught us not to cheat anyone. What is wrong will surface one day, if not today then tomorrow. You have taught us the value of our Jain way of life. It is our duty to help those in need, both by giving a helping hand and by giving alms.

Your greatest joy was always in giving. That is why you used to bring us fresh vegetables and delicious fruits.

To the world you were *kaka* ; but Kaka, you were our world
So how can we ever forget such values and such a life? We will forget all else but we will never forget such a rare and beautiful soul. We pray that wherever you are, your soul is in eternal peace.

OM SHANTI SHANTI SHANTI From your loving Family
(Speech by me at Kaka's funeral – translated from the Gujarati original)

Let us Not Forget – In loving memory of my late Father Hansraj Lakhamshi Shah (KAKA)

Thank you all attending this funeral service marking the end of one chapter in my father's life and to finally setting his soul free so that a new chapter in his life can begin.

I would like to say a few lines.
Let us not forget the sacrifices and choices he made at an early age in providing a better future for all of us.
Let us not forget his dedication to hard work for very little in return
Let us not forget his unique quality of treating everyone with respect and fairly.
Let us not forget his zest for life and his daily walks and shopping trips to buy fruit and vegetables for everyone.
Let us not forget his unreserved unselfishness
Let us not forget his passion for travelling faraway places & meeting people
Let us not forget his love of playing *bhukhar* & singing b*hajans*
Let us not forget his love of visiting people during difficult times
Let us not forget his place in this world and how he has touched everyone's hearts
Let us not forget his dedication and devotion of care to my mum
Let us not forget the special bond between our two families that he has left behind.
Let us not forget his smile and charisma and his image as the perfect gentleman
Let us not forget the undivided love he gave to all of us
Let us not forget his values and ideals of harming no one, physically, verbally or mentally
Let us not forget the love and colour he brought to everyone's life
Let us not forget his calming influence & soothing voice
Let us not forget his everlasting presence that will be in our hearts forever.
Let us not forget my father who we have all known as Kaka

Kaka, on behalf of everyone that you have known, I would like to say we are all very grateful to have known you and the effect you have had on all of us.

You have always been a father, brother, son, husband, grandfather, great grandfather or an uncle to each and every one of us and we cannot thank you enough for this love you have given us.

Thank you GOD for giving me Kaka as my father and Kaka, I have been proud to have had you as my father and may you be in eternal happiness and peace for evermore.
Kaka – I Love you very much and you will be sorely missed.
(Speech by Shailesh at Kaka's funeral)

You lived an extremely rich life full of love, honour and mutual respect. Over the years, we have observed your way of life with deep admiration.

As **a father**, you left your native homeland to provide better opportunities for your family. There is no better gift a parent can give a child. It is like planting a seed in the richest soil and the freshest water in hopes for the healthiest growth. You are a true **pioneer.**

As a **sibling**, you embraced your brother's family like it is your own. You are a **role-model** by illustrating the importance of unity. We hope to follow your example and bond our own families together for stronger relationships.

As a **grandparent**, you share unconditional love. As they say in India, the investment is more precious than the principle. Your grandchildren feel fortunate to have spent their childhoods with you. Though there is a cultural barrier due to age difference and Western customs, your grandchildren believe you are the true **hero** in the family.

As a **friend** to the *Oshwal* society, your presence is a significant one. You participated and supported community events. You have taught us that being a member of a community provides a foundation for belonging and brings out the **leader** within oneself.

Despite all these roles you have played in our lives, the most important one is the role you play as yourself. As an individual, you have found the secret to happiness by engaging in simple pleasures, spirituality, and love.
May your **soul** rest in peace.
(Speech by Monica at Kaka's funeral)

As some of you may know, *Nana* and *Nani* both had a hand in raising me and I therefore looked upon them as second parents. *Nana* was such a kind and caring person who made everyone feel as welcome as possible. He carried a great passion for music in his heart, he loved to sing and listen to others. This is where I think Uttam and I get our musical abilities from. He also loved to travel and see the world, he was such a confident man, not afraid of anything, this quality I have found in my brother Vijay who has been on various expeditions, facing extreme weather conditions.

However, the thing I think he loved the most, was to spend time with his family, talking, laughing, singing and playing *bhukhar*. Speaking on behalf of all the grandchildren who learnt how to play *bhukhar* from him, he taught us well.

To all the things that you have taught us *Nana*, I say thank you.

For the many wonderful years that I have known you, you have made my life nothing but a pleasure.
(Speech by Kavita at Kaka's funeral)

I'm very fortunate *Nana & Nani* have always been there for me and a part of the most important milestones in my life. *Nana* was there when I graduated high school, and he even picked up a few awards for me because of double bookings. They were present when I graduated from university and they were with me when I got married. And finally Jainam, the most important person and event in my life, made it to visit them. I spent my childhood summers with *Nana* and *Nani* and I have very fond memories of that time. I wanted to spend more time with *Nana* and *Nani* and that is why I decided to spend five years in UK for a work assignment. During our time together, I enjoyed going fruit and vegetable shopping with *Nana* and accompanying *Nana* and *Nani* to events at the *Oshwal* Centre. I recall feeling lonely at times while I was in Leeds and I really appreciated it when *Nana* and *Nani* took time to visit me there. Together, we went *ghar besvanu*[101], much to the amusement of Monica, who didn't understand this concept of going to sit down at someone's house, that person being someone we didn't even know. When I had my car accident, I remember feeling very fortunate to have my *Nana* spend hours sitting with me. To me he was always kind, to everyone he met, to all in our family, and especially to me. In the end there was a lot I wanted to say to him, but I didn't have the strength to tell him. For that I'm happy that Monica (and Jainam) was able to convey some of my thoughts and feelings to him. His memory will always be fresh in my mind, and I'm sure our souls will cross again.
May his soul be in peace in his next life. Om *Shanti Shanti Shanti*.
(Tribute from Raju who could not make it to the funeral)

---

[101] Visiting someone at their house

Tributes to Ba upon her death 8 April 2012

Sadadi speeches for Ba

ODE TO BA

Now that I have become one
Thank you for what you have done

I appreciate the burden you had to bear
The amount of tender loving care

That you to me have shown
I have not always known

When I was a baby and cried
You rocked me from side to side

When I was a little girl and told you my fears
You hugged me close and wiped away my tears

When I was a teenager and often in a rage
You showed vision, hope and courage

How you must have silently suffered
And I'm truly sorry for the hurt I caused

Now that I have become one
I appreciate more what you have done

And I want to say thank you
For all your love and care and I love you too.

© Hasmita Shah 8 April 2012 (Poem by me at Ba's *Sadadi*)

Thank you for all taking time out and attending Ba's *Sadadi* today. I would just like to share a few words about my Ba with you all.

Ba, Gunvantiben was born in a small village in India called Sihan on 1st January 1930. At the tender age of 16 she met a handsome young man called Hansrajbhai from another small village called Navagam in India and they were destined to get married.

Their marriage was a kind of unusual marriage in that my mother and her sister were married to my father and her brother and that the differences in height between my Ba and my father (who we all referred to as Kaka) were striking as my mother was tiny. But what she lacked in height she made up a million times over in kindness, compassion and fairness. Ba went through some very traumatic times as a young child and in the early years of her marriage. She was very devoted to her family and community and practiced Jainism as fully as possible. For more than as long as I have been born she has been on a strict one meal a day and refusing to take anything else including water outside of this one meal. She has very rarely fallen ill (or at least not complained out being ill as you and I would) and has hardly taken any medication but instead relying on the body to naturally heal itself. She was a great believer in preserving the old and made the best use of objects and did not see any sense in replacing objects that had a useful life in them.

She gave birth to five wonderful children (four daughters and a son). Although Ba was tiny she had the biggest heart anyone could wish for. She was absolutely selfless in her actions and words and always thought of the wellbeing of others before her. If she was in pain she would rather suffer in silence in order not to impose any hardship on others around her. There have been quite a few times that she has missed her one meal for the day (as she had to have that before sunset) and she did not complain once. Her strong beliefs in religion and family values meant she was a very caring mother – the best any son or daughter could wish to have.

Ba, you have done so much for all of us without asking for anything in return and please forgive me for not being there in your one time of need and able to save you or at least ease your pain. I am sorry that I was ignorant of your suffering in silence and wish I could have done much more for you. A big comfort to all of us is knowing that you are no longer in any pain but in a place of eternal happiness and have reconnected with Kaka

(Speech by Shailesh at Ba's *Sadadi*)

Funeral Speeches for Ba

My mother's name was Gunvantiben, which literally translated means full of virtues and so I would like to tell you a little about her and her virtues.

Her first virtue was a good heart and compassion and an example comes to mind. About 30 years ago we had just finished the last day of *paryushan* and asked for forgiveness from everyone. Whilst in the car returning home, suddenly a cat crossed the road and although my brother tried to avoid it, unfortunately he hit the cat. It was still alive and my mum wrapped the cat with her own shawl and cradled it all the way to the vet's reciting *navkar mantra* continuously. Unfortunately the cat did not survive and my mum was really upset that not only had we caused the death of an innocent life but that too on such an auspicious day. After this every year she would fast without fail on that day in memory of the cat and she also started to put out milk daily for the neighbours' cats. Such was her compassion that she valued all life dearly including that of this cat that she hadn't known and only held briefly in her arms for a few moments.

Her second virtue was steadfast resolve and being able to bear hardship. We had gone to Tunisia about 13 years ago and as you know she would only eat one meal a day. So that morning she had eaten her meal at around 10am so she wouldn't have to worry about food once we got there. But in the plane she was really sick and threw up for most of the journey, as well as the coach journey afterwards. She'd probably taken out more than she'd eaten in the morning. And we know she never took any water after her meal and even at this time after all she'd thrown up, she refused. The next day she was fasting and when she fasts for a day she does a complete fast without taking any food or water. So again the next day she did not take any water. So by the time she broke her fast the following lunchtime, she had gone for over 50 hours without taking in any food or water. On top of this, on the day of her fast, we walked about a couple of miles on the beach and she was happy to walk with us. So this was her ability to bear hardship and her steadfast resolve.

Her third virtue was faith – about 7 years ago, on the occasion of the opening of the *derasar* at Potters Bar, our family had the good fortune to put a *kadas* on top of the *derasar*. She was so happy that day.

9 months earlier, she had suffered a heart attack and she used to walk with a stick. But on this day, she walked without a stick up this precarious ladder. We were all worried about what would happen if she fell. But she kept insisting that nothing was going to happen to her and

that God was with her. And that day she clapped so loudly and was almost dancing with joy. So where did she get her strength from? This was her faith – her total unfaltering faith.

Her fourth virtue was her generosity towards those less fortunate – she always gave to a wide number of causes, from the needy, to the orphaned, to the disabled and even to animal welfare charities. Recently a couple of months ago, she went to *Oshwal* Centre for the first lunch gathering of the elderly (*Anand Yatra*[102])and as she was there, she decided to sponsor the event saying that she wasn't sure whether she would get this opportunity again. Also she had pledged an amount towards the Navagam reunion and it was only on Friday (2 days before she passed away) that I had given her the cheque. So this was her generosity till the end.

Then was her virtue of determination and will power. She loved her *chaas* and yogurt but after listening to a lecture on the realities of dairy farming, she decided there and then to give up milk and milk products and become a vegan. This last week she was doing her *ayambil* , but from Wednesday she was complaining of a stomach ache, so we said to her to go to the hospital but she was not wanting to break her *ayambil* and said it would ease after a few days. Her mind was made up – she was determined to finish her *ayambil*. On Saturday she agreed to go to the hospital as the pain had got worse and her *ayambil* had finished. There she celebrated the finishing of her *ayambil* with some *raab*[103] and daal *bhat*. And then on Sunday morning she passed away silently.

So this was my mother – simple, full of compassion, determined with a steadfast resolve, generous and having unwavering faith. So I also have complete and utter faith that such a devoted and pure soul will surely get eternal peace and she will look upon us fondly.

OM *SHANTI SHANTI SHANTI*
(Speech by me at funeral – translated from the Gujarati original)

---

[102] Literally - a pilgrimage of joy; it is the name for the weekly Oshwal elderly gathering
[103] Sweet soup of millet or wheat with *ghee* and jaggery

Ba was born on 1/1/1930 in Sihan, India. She was the youngest in her family, 3 older sisters and one older brother. Her early childhood was a difficult one. Her mother was deemed mentally unstable when Ba was about 3-4 years old and was kept locked up. Ba would take her food and clean up after her. Ba was 6 when her mother died. Ba was 16 when she got married and 6 months later they came to Kenya. In 1947 her first daughter Niru was born, followed by another 3 daughters, Manjula, Prafula(Bena), Hasmita (Hasu), and finally a son, Ba's family was very religious and so she never ate any root vegetables, steadfastly sticking to her principles even when she came to Kenya. Every day she would carry out her religious rituals, *darshan*, and *samayik* and would also observe fasting, *ayambils*, never eating after sunset etc. For more than the last 30 years, she decided to only eat one meal a day and only take in any water during the meal. Then around 7 years ago, she became vegan after hearing of cruelty behind dairy products. She has steadfastly observed this through her various illnesses. On 5 December 1971, the family moved from Kenya to London. Despite living in the 21st century, in a western environment, Ba continued with her strict religious observations, daily rituals and steadfast resolve. In March 1996, just a week before we were due to celebrate Ba and Kaka's Golden Wedding anniversary with much pomp and ceremony, she was taken to hospital and it turned out she had been walking on broken legs. She had to have operations on both her legs and metal plates put in. With her strong will and determination she made a full recovery. In October 2004, she had a heart attack and had to have angioplasty but again made a full recovery. For the last 5 years, she decided to stop taking all medication despite having high blood pressure, cholesterol and heart issues. After her heart surgery she still managed to visit the US to attend her first grandson's wedding as well as visiting India several times to visit her siblings and attend family weddings there. In June 2009, my dad, her partner of 63 years, passed away. This was a great loss for all the family and especially for my mum who was now even more lonely and isolated. She was determined to stay in her own home and fend for herself. She had wonderful support from her family, extended family and friends and neighbours who would bring her shopping and take her to visit people. She kept in touch with everyone by phoning them regularly – everyone we would meet would ask us how mum was and say that she had phoned them every few days. Over the last week she had been feeling a little unwell – but was determined to finish her *ayambil* and not go into hospital. Her *ayambil* finished on Friday and then on Saturday she was taken to hospital where she passed away peacefully the next morning. She leaves behind 4 daughters and one son, 12 grandchildren and 2 great grandchildren. May her soul rest in peace

Ba, as your body lies here with us waiting for us to release you from this world and onto a world filled with eternal happiness and to be re-united with your soul-mate, here are a few words that I would like you to hear now as I never had the courage to tell you when you were alive.

Ba, please forgive me for the pain and suffering that I caused you when I was ill or in pain. You would tend to my every need – you would make sure I never went hungry and you would unreservedly sacrifice your happiness for mine.

Ba, please forgive me for the burden I put on you as I have been growing up throughout the years.

Ba, please forgive me for the distress and worrying that I must have caused you when I have come home later than expected.

Ba, please forgive me for running over a cat as my actions of that tragic night 30 years ago resulted in how you conducted your life from thereafter.

Ba, please forgive me for the suffering that you have gone through with the medication during your hip plates operation.

Ba, please forgive me for not being able to do more to ease your suffering after the loss of Kaka (my dad). I now know that you have suffered in silence every day since.

Ba, please forgive me for not being able to do more in your one time of need.

Ba, although you hardly had any education you have been an inspiration to many thousands of people and you have the highest level of wisdom which no level of education can ever top.

Very few of us can claim to have a clean and pure soul, full of kindness, compassion and total devotion to the core principles that one believes in and you have all those qualities.

I am proud to be your son and will miss you dearly.

May you forever be in peace.

Om *Shanti Shanti Shanti*

A MOTHER'S LOVE

A Mother's love is something that no one can explain,

It is made of deep devotion and of sacrifice and pain,

It is endless and unselfish and enduring come what may

For nothing can destroy it or take that love away . . .

It is patient and forgiving when all others are forsaking,

And it never fails or falters even though the heart is breaking . . .

It believes beyond believing when the world around condemns,

And it glows with all the beauty of the rarest, brightest gems . . .

It is far beyond defining, it defies all explanation,

And it still remains a secret like the mysteries of creation . . .

A many splendoured miracle man cannot understand

And another wondrous evidence of God's tender guiding hand.

(Shailesh speech and poems at Ba's funeral)

A short explanation of Jainism and a brief history of Oshwals

Jainism is one of the oldest surviving religions practiced today and is still followed by millions, mainly in India. Unlike other religions, Jains don't believe in a creator God but in 24 spiritual leaders known as 'Tirthankars' of which the last two are the most well-known, Shree Parsvanath Swami and Shree Mahavir Swami. They reformed the religion to what it is today. Jains believe that the body is a house for the soul which has the capability to feel and express emotions. The soul migrates from one living form to another through the process of life and death. Whether a soul will be a plant, animal, insect, or human is determined by the good and bad deeds attached to the soul in the current and previous lifetimes. These good and bad deeds are known as 'Karma'. Jains aspire to liberate the soul from all binding karma to achieve eternal happiness. All Tirthankars have liberated their souls and thus no longer go through the cycle of birth and death. The main principles of Jainism are as follows:

- Ahimsa (Non-Violence) – To cause no harm to any living beings, intentionally or unintentionally. This goes beyond being vegetarian as it does not simply involve killing other living beings; it also involves not insulting or harming living beings through thought, actions and deeds.
- Satya (Truthfulness) – To always speak the truth.
- Asteya (Non-Stealing) – Not to take anything that is not willingly given. One should be satisfied with whatever they have earned through their own hard work.
- Aparigraha (Non-Possession) – To detach oneself from all material things.
- Brahmacharya (Celibacy) – To conquer passion and to control the senses.

Our community is the Halari Visa Oshwal community, generally shortened to the Oshwal community. The largest concentrations of Oshwals are in India, the United Kingdom and East Africa. In addition there are sizeable populations of Oshwals residing in North America, Canada and Australia.

The origin of the name "Oshwal" is probably tied to a small village called Ossiya in Rajasthan, India. It is widely accepted that our ancestors were previously from the warrior caste but converted to Jainism around 400BC. Following economic hardship and religious persecution, a small number of these peoples migrated to Sindh, now in Pakistan. The conditions in Sindh were also harsh, and they migrated to Kutch in Gujarat.

Around 1535, a small group of Oshwals of Vagad District suddenly left Kutch and moved to Saurashtra, in Gujarat. During this time, Kutch was ruled by two brothers, Jam Hamirji and Jam Rawal. As a result of internal conflict, Jam Rawal assassinated Jam Hamirji and seized the properties. Hamirji's heirs with the help of their friends defeated Jam Rawal; the latter had to flee with his followers, some of whom were Oshwals. They crossed the desert of Kutch and established a settlement around city of Khamhaliya of Halar district, naming it the capital. Later on, the settlement spread eastwards and a new capital was founded which was named after Jam Rawal as Jam Nagar. To this day, the Oshwal settlements still exist in the 52 villages between these two cities. That is why we are known as Halari Oshwals. By profession, our ancestors were mostly farmers and traders, some were moneylenders and a few were even hired hands. Many have now left the villages to settle in Jamnagar, Mumbai, Bangalore and other parts of India. Many also migrated to Africa, UK, the Americas, Australia, and other parts of Asia. The majority of the Oshwals are followers of Jain religion. Oshwals are divided into a number of groups by *attak*.

Glossary of Gujarati words

Athai - 8 days of continuous fasting only drinking boiled water – no other liquids or solids
Attak - surname. The community name for Oshwals is Shah and most use that as their surname, rather than their *attak*. Kaka was Dodhia and Ba was Jakharia
Anand Yatra - literally pilgrimage of joy; it is the name for the weekly Oshwal elderly gathering and lunch
Anna - old Indian currency equivalent to 1/16 of a rupee
Apasano - resthouse for Jain monks and nuns
Avatar - life form
Ayambil - 9 days of cleansing the body where certain foods such as oil, spices (except for salt and pepper) and vegetables and fruits are not consumed

Ba - mother
Bambo - a hot water boiling tank
Banevi - sister's husband
Banya - business
Bapuji - father
Ben - sister (also used as a suffix to a name as a mark of respect for elders)
Bestu varash - New Year
Bhabhi - brother's wife
Bhai - brother (also used as a suffix to a name as a mark of respect for elders)
Bhajan - religious song
Bhat - rice
Bhel poori - Indian savoury snack
Bhojan - meal
Bhukhar - Indian card game

Carom - Indian board game like mini snooker
Chaas - yogurt drink
Cher - leaves of trees that used to grow by the sea
Chevdo - fried Indian savoury snack
Chhakadi - Indian card game with 6 players
Chopda Poojan - religious ceremony during Diwali for closing the financial accounts
Chok - square cubicle, like a shower base without the uppers walls, for washing dishes
Chokadi - Indian card game with 4 players

Dada - paternal grandfather

Darshan - prayers
Dattan - twig used for brushing teeth – in Kenya we used the twig from acacia trees
Derasar – Jain temple
Dharamshala – religious resthouse
Daal - lentil soup
Dhokra - Indian savoury snack
Dhol - Indian drum
Diksha - renounce the world and become a monk or nun

Faiba - aunt (father's sister)
Fuva - uncle (father's sister's husband)

Ghanti - a hand mill made of stone for grinding flour
Garba - Gujarati folk dance
Ghar Besvanu – visiting someone at their house
Ghee - clarified butter
Gilli danda- outdoor game played with a short rod and a long stick

Jamvanu - gathering for the purposes of lunch or dinner
Jaan - groom's wedding party
Jalebi - deep friend Indian sweet

Kadas - golden pot
Kaka - uncle (father's brother)
Kaki - aunt (father's brother's wife)
Kavad - a long stick balanced on the shoulder with a pail at each end
Khakra - hard chapatti
Khataru - open topped truck
Koda kodi - game played by the couple after the wedding to find a ring in a plate of milk

Kshamapana -Jain forgiveness prayer usually recited at the end of a *bhajan* session.

Laaj- long veil
Lagnotri - a pre-wedding ceremony where the wedding invitation is sent from the bride's parents to the groom's parents

Mahajanwadi - community centre
Maharaj – priest who performs the wedding rituals
Mahavir Jayanti - birth of Lord Mahavir
Maitri Bhavanu - a religious song of friendship composed by an eminent Jain scholar Gurudev Chitrabhanu
Mama - uncle (mother's brother)

Mami - aunt (mother's brother's wife)
Masa - uncle (mother's sister's husband)
Masi - aunt (mother's sister)
Mandap - the pavilion for the wedding ceremony consisting of 4 pillars and a canopy
Mandhvo - pre wedding ceremony
Mandir - Hindu temple
Motabapa - paternal grandfather; *dada* is another name for paternal grandfather
Motiba - paternal grandmother; *dadi* is another name for paternal grandmother

Nagar Palika - head or mayor of town
Nana - maternal grandfather
Nani - maternal grandmother
Nasto- generic name for all snacks
Navai - 9 days of continuous fasting only drinking boiled water – no other liquids or solids
Navkar Mantra- the most important Jain prayer

Ondhwo - Indian savoury cake
Oothbes- Standing up and squatting down numerous times holding your right ear with the left hand and left ear with the right hand

Oshwal - Jain community originating from Halar in India
Otlo - A seating area in the villages, usually with a tree in the middle as in the picture of Kakabhai Sihan. This would be the centre point where people would congregate for a chat

Paise - Indian currency -100 paise in a rupee
Papad - poppadum
Paratha- fried chapatti
Paryushan - 8 day Jain festival of contemplation, reflection, fasting and forgiveness
Penda - Indian sweet made from milk and sugar
Pratikraman - prayer session to contemplate, reflect and repent
Pooja - prayer ritual

Raab - sweet soup of millet or wheat with *ghee* and jaggery
Raas - Gujarati folk dance involving sticks
Rotli- chapatti
Rotlo - millet chapatti

Saak- curry
Sadadi - prayer meeting (following a death)

Sagadi - open stove
Sakar - sugar cubes
Samayik - 48 minute prayer and meditation
Sangeet Sandhya - pre wedding fun event comprising of music, dances and speeches
Savantsari bhojan - community lunch after the end of *Paryushan*
Shanti - peace prayer
Sev - fried Indian savoury snack

Thepla - savoury chapattis

Vada - Indian savoury snack
Vidai - the parting ceremony for the bride who is leaving her family to go and live with her husband's family

Wadi - field for growing vegetables

Zambuk- medicated ointment

Swahili words

Dukas - shops

Shambas - little plots of farming land

Sources

Mau Mau uprising - sourced from Wikipedia
A short explanation of Jainism and a brief history of Oshwals - Sourced from OAUK website www.oshwal.co.uk

About the author

Although an accountant by profession, I have always enjoyed writing poems, short stories and articles for friends, family and community magazines. I have been wanting to share my parents' migration story for a while. Whilst not a unique story, I wanted to document their lives as a reminder to future generations about the sacrifices they made and the courage with which they ventured into the unknown, taking comfort from their strong principles and values. Given the current scale of migration, I think it is a particularly pertinent topic. I for one, am forever indebted to my parents for their courageous steps into the unknown and for their bold stance on education for girls.

I hope you enjoyed reading this book and it has inspired you to document your families' stories for future generations.

If you knew my parents and would like to share incidents of their life which are not reflected here, please contact me at this e-mail address: kakaandba@gmail.com

Printed in Great Britain
by Amazon